LANARKSHIRE
FOLK
TALES

To Catherine (1931-2018) and Donald Galbraith (1929-2018), my mother and father, who fostered my love of writing and telling stories.

To my sister, Marion Galbraith, who introduced me to the intriguing world of folklore when she gifted me a copy of Katharine Briggs' *British Folk Tales and Legends: A Sampler*, on my twelfth birthday.

LANARKSHIRE
FOLK
TALES

ALLISON GALBRAITH

The
History
Press

First published 2021

The History Press
97 St George's Place
Cheltenham
GL50 3QB
www.thehistorypress.co.uk

British Library Cataloguing in Publication Data.
A catalogue record for this book is available from the British Library.

ISBN 978 0 7509 7888 0

Typesetting and origination by Typo•glyphix
Printed and bound in the UK by TJ Books Limited, Padstow, Cornwall.

Trees for Lᵞfe

CONTENTS

FOREWORD

Lanarkshire is and always has been a big part of Scotland. It has towns, villages, moorland, river valleys, farms, industrial sites, gardens and orchards. Lanarkshire epitomises lowland Scotland, and continues to play a huge role in the nation's heritage and culture.

Now, in Allison Galbraith, the region has found a local storyteller able to identify and pull together the wealth of folk tales and folklore that characterises Lanarkshire north and south of the Clyde. Using the ancient 'Wards' of the county, she presents three groups of tales to tickle the ear and spice the tongue.

This book is a prime addition to the folk tale volumes produced by The History Press. It combines history and folklore, while giving prominence throughout to the voice of the storytellers. 'Wait till you hear this …'. Or as people would say in Glasgow, 'You'd better believe it.'

Allison Galbraith has filled a big gap in our storytelling literature with this fine volume. Local people will be delighted and add to the store from their own memories and experiences. For those who do not know about Lanarkshire this book will be an eye-opener. Enjoy the crack.

Donald Smith
Director, Tracs
Traditional Arts and Culture Scotland

ACKNOWLEDGEMENTS

Many thanks to Inky X for his brilliant illustrations and story map.

To Donald Smith for writing the foreword and for suggesting that I put this collection of stories together.

Respect and thanks to editor Nicola Guy for her endless patience, and to her predecessor Matilda Richards at The History Press.

A huge thank you to Alette Willis for her meticulous proof-reading and wise suggestions.

Special gratitude goes to Tessa Wyatt, artist, for her assistance.

Many historians, archivists, librarians and storytellers have supported me in my search for tales. Of these I would especially like to thank:

Paul Archibald at Lanark Library, who was extraordinarily generous with his knowledge and time.

Ed Archer, historian and archaeologist, a walking encyclopedia and force for good in Lanarkshire.

Colin McAllister, my great storytelling friend, who gave me the inspiration for the William Wallace and Marion Braidfute story.

Ewan McVicar, for his invaluable help, encouragement and support.

Alan Steele, for passing on his knowledge of Glasgow tales and showing me the importance of humour in storytelling.

Chris Ladds, for sourcing the Cora Linn story and sharing a passion for historical landscapes, wild flowers and folklore.

Jennifer Macfadyen, whose Doorstep History blog is an inspiration to anyone who wants to delve into Lanarkshire folk culture.

My friend, Robert Howat, for giving me permission to retell his mother Charlotte's family tale about Queenie the horse.

Tony Bonning, my folklore guru, for finding the Douglas stories and being wonderfully helpful.

Ian Hamilton QC, a genuine legend in his own lifetime, for giving me permission to retell his father's/family tale about the Hamiltons. And special thanks to Tommy Sherriden – another legend – for connecting me with Ian.

Anne Hunter, for giving me permission to include some of Andy Hunter's retelling of The Lee Penny.

Raymond Burke, who told me about Ms Kate Dalrymple.

Frank Miller, for my guided tour of Govan and all its treasures – if it's People that Make Glasgow, (council motto) then Frank is top of the list.

Margaret Bennet, my heroine of Scottish folklore, for her help and suggestions.

To numerous library staff, too many to mention, but particularly to the staff at Biggar Library, Angela Ward from Hamilton Library, Jenny Noble Social History Curator at Summerlee Museum of Scottish Industrial Life, Glasgow Library staff, the friendliest in the world, and Margaret McGinnty at Motherwell Library.

Paul Bristow and all at Magic Torch in Greenock, my favourite folklore friends.

Ian Wallace, for his encouragement and help at the Lanark Archives.

Simon, Mairi and Zak at Waygateshaw House, which deserves its own book of stories.

Lea Taylor, for her unwavering encouragement.

Judy Patterson, for her support and wise words.

My good friend Carol Ward, for giving me a writing retreat.

And lastly, thanks to my generous family and to Finlay Stevenson for helping me to find and explore all the locations in this book.

INTRODUCTION

This collection of folk tales and legends from Lanarkshire spirits us away on a journey around the county. They offer a very human and sometimes otherworldly glimpse of people's realities past and present. Many of the stories reflect a diverse collection of older folk beliefs and superstitions that also share similarities with ancient folk customs and beliefs found throughout Europe and in other cultures all over the world.

The county divisions and boundaries have changed many times since they were first established in the Middle Ages. Lanarkshire, situated in south central Scotland, once included: the city of Glasgow, most of East Dunbartonshire, Renfrewshire, South Lanarkshire and North Lanarkshire. Not the largest county in Scotland, but home to one fifth of Scotland's entire population, so definitely the most populated.

Currently divided into North and South Lanarkshire, with the River Clyde splitting the county neatly down the middle, the whole county resembles a triangular leaf with the Clyde as its stem. Archaeology reveals habitation from as far back as the Mesolithic era (10,000–8000 BCE) and the area was home to numerous ancient Britons and Celtic tribes. Scattered all over the land are cairns, standing stones, circles, a broch (remains in Carnwath) Bronze and Iron Age forts, Viking Hogback burial stones (one in Dalserf, five in Govan) and Roman camps, forts and roads leading to their Antonine Wall in the north. Ten

Roman legionnaires are still seen occasionally marching down Watling Street, through Crawford Village in South Lanarkshire, but only from the knees up, the bottom half of their legs lost in the sunken roads of 2,000 years ago.

The tales are divided into three sections, which reflect yet another historical division of Lanarkshire: the Upper Ward, with Lanark as its administrative centre; the Middle Ward, administered by Hamilton; and the Lower Ward, governed by Glasgow. The map and story legend provided show the boundaries of these three wards and where each tale originates from.

The stories here that contain magical or mythological beings – fairies, ghosts, a broonie, a wraith, a mermaid, witches and devils – are told to us as though they are true, making them into folk legends. Although these characters and motifs are shared across a much wider folk culture, certain tales have migrated to particular places and people, and have been absorbed into local history, becoming part of the county's cultural heritage. They have survived in the rural parishes of Lanarkshire, where calendar customs and the agricultural rhythms of the year are still part of community life. Some of these rituals and celebrations, like summer fairs and gala days, still exist. The town of Lanark celebrates its Lanimer week in June. It's an exhilarating six days of fun, when the community engage together in old customs and land rites, like the Perambulation of the Marches and the Ride-Out, which date back almost a thousand years.

In Carnwath, they hold the annual Red Hose Race, the oldest surviving footrace in the world, begun in 1508 when James IV of Scotland offered a pair of Red Hose (socks) to the person running most quickly from the east end of Carnwath to the Calla Cross – an incentive to keep soldiers fit.

There is also the New Year bonfire in Biggar, thought to be a direct descendant of a pagan fire rite to ward off evil spirits. The fire has traditionally been huge and so close to the town hall that it beggars belief; however, the old saying, 'London and

Edinburgh are big, but Biggar's Biggar' gives us a clue to the grandiose spirit of the town and its customs.

For similar reasons to Biggar's Hogmanay Bonfire, Lanark's Whuppity Scoorie ritual, on 1 March (included in the Lanark chapter), literally whips the bad spirits out of town.

While the villages and towns in South Lanarkshire have kept some form of annual community celebration alive, it has been harder for the industrialised northern part of the county to hang on to its folk customs, and also more difficult to find folk tales or legends from North Lanarkshire.

Because most of the region lies on top of coalfields and iron deposits, Lanarkshire became home to the iron industry of the nineteenth century. Something about the process of industrialisation in the north (the middle and lower wards), where the steel industry was located, seems to have broken the folk memory of stories and tradition. Migrant workers who came to work in the county would have brought their own stories and customs with them, and so many of the indigenous Lanarkshire tales faded from memory. There are only three folk tales included in this collection from North Lanarkshire, which probably survived because they were connected to specific features in the landscape. Maggie Ramsay, a witch who haunted the North Burn in Airdrie, was linked to a huge boulder in the burn. The rock is no longer there, but the place was once called 'Fiddle Naked' and its association with witches appears to go back much further than the eighteenth century when Maggie's story was circulating. Another tale, about a family curse, was attached to a glen in Monklands, once known as Lover's Loup (Leap), which is also gone, the glen having been used as an in-fill site for the by-products of coal mining. The third tale is about Bartram de Shotts, a man of giant stature who terrorised the road to Glasgow and Edinburgh. It is associated with St Catherine's Well, near Kirk O' Shotts. The well is still there, a real, physical presence in the landscape, which has helped to preserve the folk memory of Bartram's legend.

When heavy industries dig, scar and destroy the natural features of the land they appear to take most of the old stories away with them.

Along with the fairy tales, I have included legends of William Wallace and Marion Braidfute, King Robert the Bruce, the Black Douglas, Kings and Queens of the early Brythonic Kingdoms and Lailoken, the most compelling candidate for a real, historical Merlin. Stories migrate and change over many millennia, like the story about Sir Douglas who, while sheltering under a tree in Douglasdale, watched a wyver (spider) spinning her web in a branch above his head, and then took strategic battle inspiration from the spider's tenacity. Over time and retelling, this story metamorphosed into the tale of Bruce and the Spider. Rumour has it that Sir Walter Scott was the first to swap the protagonists' names, but maybe that's just as well, as the story has survived seven hundred years and is still ours for the telling.

Like the folk tales of North Lanarkshire, the folk stories of Glasgow have largely been lost to industrialisation and the huge evolutionary tides of human migration (my own family included). There are hundreds of stories about the city and its inhabitants from the last couple of centuries, but they mostly fall into the ghostly and crime categories. However, I did unearth enough stories from Glasgow that I would enjoy telling at social gatherings and have included them in the Lower Ward section. The oldest are about Saint Kentigern, or St Mungo, as he is better known. Some of his miracles are related on the Glasgow Coat of Arms, which once bore the motto, 'Let Glasgow flourish by the Preaching of the Word and Praising Thy Name', now shortened to 'Let Glasgow Flourish'. This motto relates to one of Mungo's miracles: while preaching a sermon to a crowd near the Molendinar Burn, the ground rose up beneath him, so that he was elevated high enough for the people to see and hear him. Legends of saints preserved in the early hagiographies have remained popular, celebrated by people regardless of their faith, stories that share the myth and magic of the place to which they belong. Through the stories of Mungo and his miracles, people seem to relate proudly to the city; these old legends giving a rich connection to a distant past in the living present. This demonstrates the power of the oral tale to transcend time and influence us. While presenting a storytelling workshop at a Flood Defence conference in Glasgow, I told a watery Mungo legend – milk gifted by Mungo to an employee is accidentally spilled into the River Clyde, it is not washed away, but churned by the waves and propelled back out of the water, as blocks of miraculous cheese!

Stories are a well-proven, effective way to entertain and educate people, as well as to make saints.

The only tale collected directly from an oral history source, the Black Clydesdale Horse, comes from the cultural life of the county, reminding us of a time in history when this iconic horse breed was as important as the motor industry is today; a time that has now passed, but deserves its place in folk memory. Like the last story in this collection, the Vampire with the Iron Teeth, a real happening reported on all over the world. It proves conclusively that folklore and folk tales are being created in tandem with our existence, the places we live, the activities we enjoy and the stories we choose to share with each other – we are the folk!

There is something peculiar about the nature of folk tales, perhaps created by the act of passing them from teller to listener, into literary sources, then back to the tellers and listeners, over many lifetimes. Sometimes they are forgotten and lost, never to be heard again. Others are rediscovered in old books, songs, newspapers and pamphlets, their magic and wisdom accessible to us once more; like a few of the rare finds in this collection. These stories are multi-generational, suitable for adults and children alike, and even better when shared by young and old together. Perhaps not for younger children though, as some of the tales are too gruesome – Inky X, the illustrator for *Lanarkshire Folk Tales*, commented that he'd drawn 'Three decapitated heads in one week!' An inevitable, bloody consequence of historical legends.

This book is for storytellers, readers and listeners who revel in hearing about the journeys our ancestors took and the stories they brought back with them. I hope you enjoy and pass them on in turn.

Dragon/Dog
sculpture on Cardell
Hall, Govan, Glasgow.

About the Author

Allison Galbraith has lived in Lanarkshire, Scotland, for over thirty years. While working in the performing arts she began telling stories professionally for Glasgow Libraries in 1992.

Completing a Masters degree in Scottish Folklore in 2012, she co-wrote her first collection of folk tales with Alette Willis, *Dancing with Trees, Eco-Tales from the British Isles*, The History Press, 2017.

About the Artist

Inky X is quite simply a genius. You can find him at www.inkyx.com

Story Map of Lanarkshire Folk Tales:

Upper Ward
1. Cowdaily Castle – Carnwath
2. Michael Scot and his Industrious Imps – Carnwath
3. The Brownie of Dolphinton Mill – Dolphinton
4. Murder on Libberton Moor – Libberton
5. The Fairies of Merlin's Crag – Biggar
6. The Oldest Man in Scotland – Leadhills
7. Fairy Tales from Douglas – Douglas
8. Nannie's Invisible Helper – Douglas
9. The Legend of Cora Linn – Lanark
10. Stories and Folklore from Lanark's Castlegate – William Wallace and Marion Braidfute, Whuppity Scoorie, The Girnin Dog – Lanark
11. Wallace and the Wraiths of Clydesdale – Kirkfieldbank
12. Katie Neevie's Hoard – Lesmahagow
13. The Lockharts' Lucky Penny – Lanark
14. The Black Clydesdale Horse – Carluke

Middle Ward
15. The Blue Flame of Strathaven – Strathaven
16. Sita, the Indian Princess of Larkhall – Larkhall – Hamilton
17. The Cadzow Oaks – Cadzow – Hamilton

18. The Curling Warlock of Mains Castle – East Kilbride
19. Tibbie, the Witch of Kirktonholme – East Kilbride
20. The Tale of Kate Dalrymple – East Kilbride
21. Bartram, the Giant of Shotts – Kirk O' Shotts
22. The White Hare – Old Monkland
23. Maggie Ramsay: The Witch of Auld Airdrie – New Monkland/Airdrie

Lower Ward
24. The Rutherglen Bannock – Rutherglen
25. Saint Kentigern, the Patron Saint of Glasgow – Glasgow
26. How Mungo Came to Glasgow – Glasgow
27. The Battle between Morken and Kentigern – Glasgow
28. The Fish and the Ring – Hamilton
29. The Witches of Pollok – Cathcart
30. The Sheep's Heid – Govan
31. The Govan Cat – Govan
32. The Vampire with the Iron Teeth – Glasgow

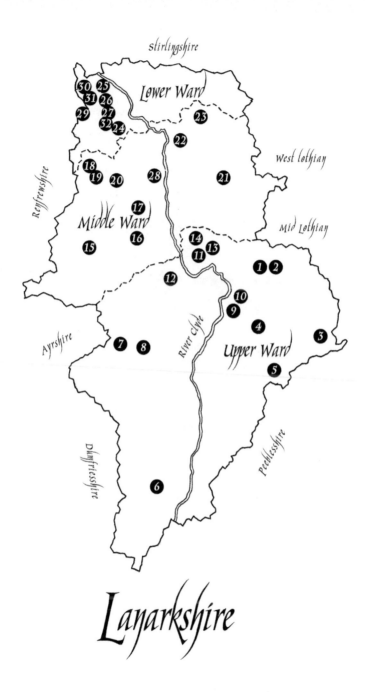

Stirlingshire

Lower Ward

30 25
31 26
29 27
32 24

23

22

West Lothian

Renfrewshire

18
19 20 28

21

Mid Lothian

17

Middle Ward

16

14
11 13

15

1 2

12

10
9

4

3

River Clyde

7 8

Upper Ward

5

Ayrshire

Peeblesshire

Dumfriesshire

6

Lanarkshire

THE UPPER WARD

COWDAILY CASTLE

The Douglas family built the original Couthally Castle in the 1100s – a strong single-tower fort on the edge of a moss about a mile north-west of Carnwath. Sir Douglas was fond of feasting and enjoyed a good party. Thanks to these frequent celebrations, the local farmers, castle servants, brewers, cooks and gardeners were kept very busy supplying the food. Almost daily, the butcher slaughtered cattle, diced their parts and loaded the fresh meat on to a cart destined for the castle kitchen. This earned Couthally the affectionate nickname of Cowdaily Castle.

During the turbulent years when Robert the Bruce and his supporters were fighting the Balliol and the English King, the castle was burned down by Lord Somerville, who claimed the ruins of this once grand fort of the Douglas clan as his prize.

Cowdaily Castle had been burned to the ground, leaving only part of the tower standing, so Lord Somerville ordered the men of Carnwath – who were now subject to him – to pull down what was left. When all that remained were a few blocks of granite and a giant mound of rocks, Somerville arrived to view the demolished site. He rode his horse around the moss and hillside accompanied by his advisor, searching for the best place to build a new castle. Finally, Somerville settled for a good location near to the original, but with even better views of Tinto and the other hills to the south.

The next day, Lord Somerville's foreman gathered a few reluctant men at the market cross. When he had enough workers, he sent them off towards the moss. As they trudged past the thatched houses of Carnwath, an old hen wife looked out from her door, raised a bony finger at them and cackled a warning.

'Yea'll get no work finished up there on yon brae, for that ground and those stones are cursed by the Douglas clan. Aye, Douglas had a pact wi the Deil himself and no good will come to any that go agin them.'

After hearing the old wyfie's warning, a few of the lads were too scared to go on. The foreman growled at them, making it clear that Lord Somerville would do far worse to them than the Devil ever could if they didn't 'Get oan wi it, and rebuild his castle.'

The men and boys worked hard shifting stones and rocks from the old castle site to the new location. Foundations were dug and giant slabs of flat stones were laid – fast progress was made on the first day of building. During the night, however, an eerie fog descended on the hillside and unearthly noises could be heard emanating out of it. The men on watch at the building site fled in terror. They ran back towards their homes, stumbling through tough tussocks of moorland grass and falling into deep bogs along the way. They arrived back to their wives and mothers, bedraggled, pale and shaking. Kettles were boiled to make hot reviving tea and drams of whisky served to calm the nerves of the spooked men. The old hen wife heard the commotion in the street and, muttering an incantation to herself, she lit a sprig of dried sage and carefully blew the smoke from the herb about her windows, the door, and up the chimney, so that no evil could enter her home.

The next morning, the villagers were up with the sunrise and out on doorsteps with their neighbours discussing the strange events of the previous evening. It was an angry, red-faced foreman, accompanied by two of Somerville's armed henchmen, who arrived at the cross that morning to round up builders for the day. Under the threat of being flogged, imprisoned, or both, the local men were given no other option than to go back to work on the castle foundations. When they arrived back at the site where they had laboured so hard the day before, the group were shocked speechless at what they saw – all of their building work had been destroyed. The huge squares of stone had been wrenched from the newly laid foundations and scattered over the hillside. Men slumped to the ground, the blood drained from their faces and their legs weak with fear. Many chanted blessings for protection, while others prayed for forgiveness for betraying their previous lord. Each man remembered the old woman's prophesy, and now they all believed it was true.

When news reached Lord Somerville about the vandalism of his building endeavours, he was furious. His immediate suspicion was that the men of Carnwath must still be loyal to their old lord and not to him, assuming that they had pulled everything down during the night. When he arrived on the scene and saw for himself how extensive the destruction was, he threatened the men with instant death if they did not begin rebuilding immediately. No one dared to protest their innocence, as they could see that the enraged lord was ready to commit murder if anyone disobeyed him.

All day long and late into the next night, the men worked without a break to rebuild what had been undone. Before midnight, they dragged their tired bodies home to their own beds, ignoring the foreman's threats of instant sacking if they left the site. The eldest of the workers told the foreman that there was nothing he could do or say to make them stay in that cursed place overnight. Fear of the Devil and what he could do to them was definitely now far greater than the fear of what any man would do to them, even if he was a lord!

The tired group of workers who arrived on the hill the next morning were greeted by a scene of even worse destruction than the day before. This time, Somerville and his henchmen were already storming through the carnage – churned earthworks and boulders strewn around the hillside.

As the men pleaded, declaring their innocence on their mothers' and children's lives', something rang true with Somerville. He'd seen how tired they had been the prior evening, clearly incapable of any further strenuous exercise. Also, he had arranged for two watchmen to sit guard on the road leading to the site. The watchmen swore that no one had approached from the village. However, they reported that they had heard strange and unnatural sounds, and had seen lightning coming from the castle area. Convinced by the wretched villagers' protests and his spies' odd report, Somerville decided that he would personally spend the next evening on the hillside, keeping watch for himself.

After the third day of work was completed, the Carnwath workmen were sent home to their village. Somerville and several armed men made camp next to the building site. They sat around a fire, drinking mulled wine, eating roast boar and joking gallusly about the ignorant and superstitious peasants.

At first, they thought nothing of the steel-grey mist that came swirling out of the darkness from the direction of the moss, entwining itself around the partly built castle walls. The fog brought a deep chill to their camp and the men pulled their woollen blankets closer around them and threw more logs on to the fire. Then, from out of the strange, icy fog came an ear-splitting screech, followed by snarls and howls, as though a giant wolf was tearing some inhuman prey into pieces. The startled men leaped to their feet just as the first of the gigantic foundation stones hurtled through the air, travelling past their heads with the velocity of a meteor. More boulders followed, coming in volleys of six, eight, ten rocks at a time and landing between the men and the brow of the hill.

Somerville pulled out his sword and rushed towards the mist and mayhem. However, the eerie ethers wrapped around his legs, his arms and torso, rendering his limbs immobile. He stood paralysed, turning to see that his men were also caught fast. Then, the most terrifying sight appeared before them. As if levitating in a halo of bright, burning dust was the Devil himself. He was cavorting among five enormous demons, ordering each of them to pull down the newly built walls. The sinister demons hurled the granite boulders through the air as easily as if they were playing a game of bowls.

Auld Nic, the Devil, turned his eyes towards Somerville and his men and laughed, sending an explosive jet of bright flame towards them. Each man collapsed, rendered senseless by the sulphuric smog that engulfed them. As they lay helpless on coarse grass and cold earth, they heard the hellish demons chanting:

Tween the Rae-hill and Loriburnshaw,
There ye'll find Cowdaily wa', [wall]
And the foundations laid on Ern. [Iron]

When each of the stones from the castle wall had been scattered about the surrounding countryside, the terrifying apparitions and their master, the Devil, disappeared back into the fog. The building work was completely destroyed. All that was left was the smell of scorched grass, sulphur and the frightened men. After many dazed minutes had passed they gathered their wits about them and returned to their lodgings in the village.

Following this experience, and very puzzled by the rhyme that the demons had chanted, Somerville asked for guidance from the local worthies and clergy. None of them could give a satisfactory answer, but one superstitious priest did have the wit to remember the hen wife's warning. The old woman was summoned. She explained to him that the original castle's foundations had been built on iron stone, and this had kept the place safe from the Devil's tricks. If the new lord truly wished to live in Carnwath, then he must build his castle on the same spot as the old one, on the bedrock of iron stone. If he did not do this, she warned, then the Devil would come back with his wicked demons and torment the lord forever.

Somerville took the wise wife's advice. He built his magnificent new castle on the original castle's foundation. Not to be outdone by the Douglas clan, Somerville added an extra tower to his fortification – a tower made entirely of stone rich in iron. It was common knowledge, at this time, among the rich and the poor alike, that iron keeps demonic and wicked

forces at bay. Although the ordinary folk couldn't afford to build with ironstone like the rich and powerful Douglas and Somerville families, they made good use of iron nails in their home's foundations and walls, and every house and barn had a horseshoe nailed to the door for protection against the Devil and his demons.

Note: The castle is now only a ruin, north-west of Carnwath.

2

MICHAEL SCOT AND HIS
INDUSTRIOUS IMPS

Nearly every county in Scotland and Northern England has a story about Michael Scot, the infamous wizard of the north. He was a real person, reputedly born at Balwearie Castle in Fife. Highly educated and a great European scholar of his time (1175–1232), Michael studied philosophy, mathematics and astrology at Durham, Oxford and Paris. He travelled widely, working for the Holy Roman Emperor Frederick II as court physician, philosopher and astrologer in Palermo, as well as translating Aristotle from Arabic to Latin.

Although the real Michael was said to have condemned magic in his writing, his connection with esoteric works, Arabic culture and astrology earned him the reputation of being involved with the dark arts, so that within one generation of his death, he was known throughout folk culture as a sorcerer and wizard.

Long ago, in the thirteenth century, the famous Scottish wizard Michael Scot arrived in Lanarkshire and decided to make some improvements to the landscape. Firstly, he wanted to put a large tract of marshy ground, just east of the town of Biggar, to better use. Michael's ambitious plan was to divert the course of the River Clyde, straight through the unproductive marshland, and into the River Tweed. What a spectacular difference this would make to the people of Clyde and Tweedsdale and to the geographical topography of Scotland. But, more importantly to Michael, this would provide the most splendidly challenging and strenuous employment for his workers.

Now, they were not ordinary men or women that laboured for him, but rather imps and sprites who belonged to the lesser class of demons. Michael had been given the arduous task of keeping this riotous army of imps busy, forever. It was impossible to know how many there were exactly as they were never stationary for long enough to count them all. They were always cavorting, cartwheeling and somersaulting through the air, or jigging, tumbling, disappearing at will, and occasionally bursting into minor explosions of fireworks and flame. There were so many of them that even Michael could not remember their names, or even tell them apart by their wicked, demon-like faces. Three of these creatures had higher status and were clearly the leaders of the pack. Their names were Prig, Prim and Pricker. They were the only ones who spoke directly to Michael.

He had to find continuous work for all of them, or they would get up to terrible deeds, upsetting people and beasts. The wizard had earned this unenviable role, as director of demons, on his twenty-first birthday. His mother, who was reputed to be a mermaid from the River Clyde, had gifted him a sorcerer's almanac. Once young Michael had absorbed the taboo knowledge of the arcane arts from the great book and began practising the secret lore and dark craft contained therein, the Devil himself had released the multitude of minor daemons to assist Michael Scott until his dying day!

For the first stage of Michael's landscaping venture, he instructed the imps to build a stone bridge over the River Clyde at Covington. The local people of the neighbouring parishes of Carnwath and Libberton were excited at the prospect of the bridge, which would make their journeys to the market at Biggar so much safer and faster. All these folk knew about the huge road improvements Michael and his unholy army had made throughout Scotland; sturdy bridges and roads, where nothing but marsh and bogs had once existed. They knew that it was thanks to the wizard's power over the hellish minions that Great Watling Street had been built along the spine of the country, connecting the far counties of England all the way up to Lanarkshire and beyond.

Michael gave the orders to his three chief sprites, Messrs Pricker, Prim and the most objectionable of the three, Prig, to use the stone from a nearby outcrop of rock – the Yelpin Craigs, a few miles from Carnwath – to build the bridge at Covington, just north of Thankerton. The unruly multitude of supernatural creatures trekked day and night from Yelpin Hill, carrying huge boulders with which to construct the bridge. There were numerous squabbles among this heathen army. Insults were hurled at whichever imp had offended its neighbour and rocks followed, sometimes smacking their target, causing injury and often concussion. Prig was usually in the midst of the argument, making sure that there was always a convenient gorse bush or thorn tree for the unfortunate imp victim to land in.

Then, quite unexpectedly one day, as the sprites were labouring up and down with their heavy loads, the news reached them that their master Michael Scot had died – poisoned by his own wife! Overjoyed, the imps each threw down their rocks and boulders. They danced and gambolled about the moor, howling and squealing for joy. Many exploded with delight, showers of sparks lighting up the countryside, as each little sprite blew like a miniature volcano. Now they were free from their servitude to the wizard. No more hard labour building roads and bridges. At last they could go back to serve their true master, the Devil, and cause mayhem and chaos wherever they chose. The delirious demons all scattered far and wide, each choosing their own particular brand of devilry; whether it was horse scaring, egg smashing, or the numerous varieties of bad luck and ill health to which humans are prone, you could be sure that one of these imps was behind the suffering.

This is why the River Clyde never was diverted from its natural course through the Clyde Valley to the marsh near Biggar, and into the River Tweed. And also, the reason why the bridge at Covington was never built. Those rocks, however, that the imps dropped when they quit their job, form a line of boulders from Yelpin Craigs, towards the river. Folk said back then that it made an imposing road of rocks, 3 miles broad, like a giant's causeway. Over the many hundreds of years since the sprites dumped their workload on the moor, farmers have gone to great expense to remove the boulders from the land. Many good stone dykes and buildings are the result of this natural, or perhaps supernatural resource. You can still see a few of these demon-scattered rocks along the moorland at Stanemuir. The Yelpin Craigs are a wild and peaceful location to visit, where you can walk among the fabled landscape, enjoying the sweet, moorland air and beautiful views of South Lanarkshire.

3

THE BROWNIE OF DOLPHINTON MILL

Dolphinton is a village and parish located in the beautiful, curva-ceous Pentland Hills on the boundary of South Lanarkshire, 7 miles north-east of Biggar, 27 miles south-west of Edinburgh. The local manor belonged in the twelfth century to Dolfine, elder brother of the first Earl of Dunbar. The Scottish brownie, or broonie, is an enigmatic, helpful spirit often attached to farms and mills. In England they were known as hobs or hobgoblins.

The Earl of Dunbar and his wife, Lady Dunbar, lived comfort-ably at their fort-alice – manor house – near to the village of Dolphinton in South Lanarkshire. The couple had been lucky enough to raise their family during peaceful times, so they were happy and contented. The big house was run as well as could be with an army of busy domestics – cooks, maids and manservants – looking after the family, the house, and all of the regular guests who came to visit the picturesque Lanarkshire home. Like all early medieval fort-alices, the manor house was almost entirely self-sufficient, with servants employed to run the farm, vegetable garden, vinery, doocots, stables and mill. However, there was one helper about the property that not all 'big-hooses' were lucky enough to have, and that was the brownie who lived there.

This brownie, or 'broonie' as he was called locally, had, as far as anyone could remember, always been there. He had come with the property. Broonies were not all that common in Scotland, but there were enough of them about, attached to farms, mills and big houses, that everyone knew a little about them and accepted them as a natural part of country life. The broonie of Dolphinton was typical of his race – he was small and wiry, with leathery skin and dark hair. He was so shy of human contact that he only ever came out at night, when occasionally, if the moon was bright enough, people might get a glimpse of him making his way across the mill yard. He worked hard for many hours every night in the mill, threshing and grinding the oats, barley and wheat. The Dunbars' miller was grateful to have such a dedicated labourer. He left a candle in a glass lamp for the 'Old Hob' – as he called him – to work by, and made sure that no servants ever disturbed the broonie during the hours from dusk till dawn. He knew that the broonie would not stand for any human company or interference in his job, but it was also wise not to let folk get a good look at the wee wrinkly old man, as it was said that these strange beings were terribly ugly, like dried up old leather boots, with bulging eyes and blackened teeth. The miller didn't want any of the rest of the staff being frightened by the sight of this poor old soul.

Treating a broonie in the correct way was always a problem for the households to which they attached themselves. Give them too much kindness and they would leave in disgust; don't give them enough respect and the same thing happened, the broonie would quit his job and never be seen in that place again. The Dolphinton broonie had appeared to be contented with his wages since the house had been built. The first miller's wife had known much about the old ways and the lore of the broonie and had struck the balance just right. Her knowledge had been passed on to the second generation to run the farm and mill, and they had been careful to follow her instruction: 'Broonie must have a cup of milk and oaten bannock left out for his supper every night.' The cup was always empty and the bannock gone by morning, so everyone trusted that this was what the broonie liked. As no one ever actually spoke with him, though, this was just an assumption, and if the old brownie had wanted something more from his employer, they would never have known. This thought occurred to Lady Dunbar one day and she called on the miller's wife to discuss the matter with her.

Being the second millers to work at Dolphinton Manor, this particular miller's wife was not so up on the law of supernatural helpers like fairies and broonies. She asked her husband to tell her all he knew about broonies and then she asked the older folk at market that week. Each one had a different opinion about broonies and their habits. Some said to 'Never give them more', and others thought a 'Suit of new clothes at Whitsuntide each year' was acceptable. Mostly, she heard familiar tales of the helpful spirits taking terrible offence when gifts, or better food rations, were provided. Each story ended with the broonie becoming very upset and quitting his job! The miller's wife reported all of this back to the earl's wife. Lady Dunbar was delighted at so much information, but equally perplexed about what to do for their hard-working broonie. After much discussion, the two women agreed that it was not a good idea to give him more milk, or put butter, or honey on his bannock, his rations should stay the same as they were, but maybe he was due a new set of clothes. It had been over twenty years since the previous miller's wife had made a mantle and hood for their good little man, so the two women concluded that a new outfit should be acceptable to him by now.

The Lady of Dolphinton, the miller's wife and the housekeeper were up very early the next morning preparing themselves for a day out to the nearest big town. The housekeeper's husband hitched the horses to the coach and drove the excited party seven miles south to Biggar. Here they spent a long, indulgent day visiting the marketplace and almost every shop in the town and eating a much-needed lunch at the Crown Inn. The women were spoiled for choice as they perused all kinds of fancy goods, linens, wool, flax, local foods and crafts. When they returned home that evening, the carriage was weighed down with their purchases. All three slept soundly along the bumpy highway, exhausted by their shopping extravaganza. The next morning, the new bolts of cloth were laid upon the kitchen table and a committee of servants was invited to help Lady Dunbar choose the correct material for the broonie's new clothes. Fine lambswool dyed ochre and russet, Irish linen in duck-egg blue, or Hebridean plaid in shades of heather and moss – which one would be best for the little night worker of Dolphin' Mill? Each of the servants was consulted for an opinion, and each argued a case for the textile they preferred. A final vote was cast and the smooth, duck-egg blue linen was chosen as the favourite. The shears were brought to the table and lengths of cloth cut to the correct size for the small man – who was no bigger than a child of five or six years old, but had the strength of at least three men!

Sewing was just commencing when Lord Dunbar looked in on the throng of chattering women gathered by the fireside in his kitchen. Curtsies were bobbed, as maids and servants jumped respectfully to their lord's attendance. He stood in amazement at the scene of domestic co-operation before him. At the table, his wife held court among the servants, a large needle and thread in her hand. She explained to him what they were doing, and he laughed until tears ran down his face. In fact the lord laughed so hard that he had to sit down in an oaken settle by the fire and be given a warm drink with a nip of brandy. He called for the miller to come and enjoy the occasion, too. The miller was aghast when he arrived and saw what his wife and the serving women were up to. The earl poured his mill man a dram of brandy, to help appease his concern. The miller explained that this was a mistake to offer a broonie such fine clothes and especially in such a dandy 'hue of blue'! He insisted that this was the type of misguided kindness that offended and upset the little men, and that their hard-working broonie would leave them the moment he set eyes on the gift of clothes that were being made.

Finally, it was agreed by the now very merry throng of folk in the kitchen – warmed brandy had been slipped into flasks and beakers of milk and enjoyed by all – that whatever they did, they must not offend the broonie. The expensive Irish linen was put aside and two sacks of hemp, which had stored oats, were found instead. These were shaken empty, the remaining grain dust was beaten from them, and then they were cut to shape and sewn in the very latest fashion. Each servant took a turn at stitching, handing the work to the next person when they realised that they could no longer see or sew straight due to intoxication. Eventually, a fine short tunic, baggy hose and hooded mantle were completed. Everyone agreed that it was a unique and splendid outfit. If they had been a little more honest and a lot more sober they would have admitted that the sackcloth was too rough to be worn against skin. But they made slurred excuses that this was for the wee broonie, and coarse hemp would be very durable at night in the mill.

That evening, as the miller's wife took down the usual bowl of milk and oaten biscuit to leave for their best worker, the lady of the house came carrying the parcel of new clothes. Many of the household's servants followed them to the barn, or watched from the windows and doors of the manor house. The onlookers smiled at the thought of how happy the wee old broonie would be when he saw his suit of rustic new clothes. The mistress put them on a wooden box next to the lamp. Then she and the miller's wife hid themselves in the storage room next to the threshing barn. The miller was sent 'To guard the women from fright,' by the earl, who had retired to bed earlier with a sore head.

When the brownie arrived for his evening's labour, he stopped at the barrel where his food awaited him. He drank down his milk and began to munch on his bannock, but as he ate he noticed the bundle of hempen cloth beside the candle. Grunting a little, he poked the bundle and the hose fell down to the ground. Broonie stooped to pick them up muttering and cursing as he bent his stiff, old back. The ladies hiding and watching the scene were tense with excitement, trying to hold their breath so that they would make no noise. While the wee man inspected the short sackcloth trousers that he'd just picked up, he began to splutter, as it dawned on him that the clothes lying next to his supper were meant for him. He grabbed the tunic then the hood, he looked at them for a moment then threw the whole lot down to the ground. Stamping furiously, the broonie moaned a long howl, like an animal in pain. He kicked the new clothes across the barn and cried out angrily:

> Sin' ye've given me a harden ramp,
> Nae mair of your corn I will tramp.

With a final curse and a look of disgust at the pile of sackcloth clothes now scattered across the room, the wee old man shook his head sadly and stomped away out of the barn. He disappeared across the yard into the night and was never seen at the mill, or in the Dolphinton district ever again.

The miller and household were sad to see him go and the family, especially Lady Dunbar, were terribly upset that they had chosen the wrong cloth to make a new suit for their helpful broonie.

4

MURDER ON LIBBERTON MOOR

In the churchyard of Libberton is an old gravestone that has engraved upon it the story of the heartless murder of Adam Thomson in 1771. It is a true story of a son's exceptional detective work as he hunted for his father's killers.

Between Biggar and Carnwath, Adam Thomson and his wife lived in a cottage, on the windswept moors. They were an affable and hard-working older couple, well-liked locally. Adam made a fair living, making and selling heather besoms, rush mats and baskets. He was so highly skilled in such hand-weaving crafts that his goods were always in great demand at local markets. It wasn't enough to make him rich though, especially as every penny they could afford was saved to pay for their son's education. This thrifty approach paid off very well, as Adam Junior passed his school exams and in time was employed as the schoolmaster at nearby Walston School.

It is believed that word spread amongst rival market hawkers and travelling traders that the old couple were so comfortably off that they had a fortune in money hidden about their house.

On a summer's night in July 1771, the couple were wakened by loud hammering on their door. Adam went to see who was calling at such a late time and as he opened the door, two men knocked him to the ground and stabbed him through the heart. Old Adam died instantly, on his own doorstep. The assailants went on to attack his wife, knock her unconscious and ransack the house for everything – what little there was – of value.

The alarm was raised locally, and the surrounding parishes were greatly shocked, saddened and frightened by such a heinous, cold-blooded crime. Several rewards were offered for the capture of, or information about, the murderer or murderers, but sadly nothing came of it.

Young Adam made up his mind that he would find his father's killers. He knew that he could not get any peace of mind until they were brought to justice. There was no police force as we know it today, so he had to take matters into his own hands and look for the killers himself.

Adam Junior began his search up and down the country. He accepted lifts from kindly carters and carriages when offered, but mostly he walked the length and breadth of Scotland on foot. He went to every place where lowlifes and criminals frequented. This included bars, inns, brothels, gambling houses and gaols. He went to town and city courtrooms to talk with accused and convicted criminals. He even pretended to be a pickpocket, thief and highway robber, just to get accepted in underground gangs, in order to glean any information he could on the men who had murdered his father.

His detective work continued for many months, taking him into the company of the most depraved individuals in the country. He travelled throughout Scotland and England, following false leads, and dubious clues, until exhausted and completely disheartened, he returned home to Lanarkshire.

After going to bed one evening, he lay with his restless mind tracing over all the journeys and the many scoundrels he had met on his hellish travels, when a mysterious voice whispered quietly, 'Arise and search.' Adam wasted no time setting off again the next morning. He followed his gut instinct and headed east towards Jedburgh.

When he was allowed to talk among the prisoners in Jedburgh Tolbooth, he spoke with a vagrant man who told him about some rough gypsy types who had spoken about killing an old man and his wife, from up the Lanarkshire way. And although they hadn't found much money for their troubles, they boasted that they'd put a basket maker, better skilled than any of them, out of business once and for all. This was the vital clue that Adam had been looking for, which ultimately led to the arrest of two men and two women at Inversnaid.

John Brown and James Wilson were put on trial in Edinburgh on 12 August 1773 for the murder of Adam Thomson. The two women, Martha and Janet, who had been with them on the fateful night, and witnessed the crime, were not charged, as they had turned King's evidence.

The jury's verdict was swift and unanimous. The men were condemned to be executed in the Grassmarket in Edinburgh on 15 September and their bodies given to Dr Monro for dissection.

On the day of their execution, Adam Thomson accompanied them on to the scaffold and prayed peacefully for the salvation of their souls.

Adam's detective work and diligence had been remarkable throughout the one and a half years it had taken him to find the murderers and bring them to justice. He had the circumstances of his father's death inscribed on a tombstone, with the killers' names included, and then erected in Carnwath Churchyard. Then Adam returned to his teaching job at the school in Walston, where he lived happily and peacefully, passing on the gift of learning to many generations of local children. For years, people came from near and far to see the unusual gravestone. And if your curiosity likewise brings you to South Lanarkshire to read Adam Thomson's moving inscription, then you'll have to visit Libberton Kirkyard, to where Adam's nephew had the stone removed, to be at final peace and rest with his mother (the murdered man's sister) Elizabeth Thomson.

5

THE FAIRIES OF
MERLIN'S CRAG

An early version of the Fairies of Merlin's Crag, by Elizabeth
Grierson, 1910, sets the story in Lanarkshire, but an even earlier
version in W.W. Gibbings' collection from 1889 does not mention
the county, only that it happened at Merlin's Craig. There is no place
called Merlin's Craig in Lanarkshire, but there is a Merlindale near
Broughton, in the Borders, the county next to South Lanarkshire.
And there are many legends from this area about a castle where
Merlin is said to have lived and about his death and burial place
*at the Powsail Burn, near Drumellzier. (*Finding Merlin – The
Truth Behind the Legend, *by Adam Ardrey, 2013.)*

Maybe this tale does not truly belong to Lanarkshire, but as it
has been retold so often as a Lanarkshire story, I am happy to carry
on the tradition and include it in this collection.

Wullie Hannah worked as barnman (odd-job man), doing
whatever was needed in and around the farms near his home in
Lanarkshire. The local farmers liked him well enough and kept
him in regular employment, which was a good thing for Wullie
and his wife, because they had plenty of bairns to feed, clothe
and keep warm in their wee, but'n ben house.

One day, Wullie was working for a farmer who had sent him to cut peat turfs from the hillock above his farm. The rise of land was known locally as Merlin's Crag – a rocky outcrop at the top of an oddly curved hillside. It was said to have been a magical place where the great bard Merlin had studied the stars and comets in a time long past. These legends had been handed down, word of mouth, by many generations and it was common belief among ordinary folk that this was a fairy hill. Wullie hadn't ever given this much thought, it was just a name to him, and he certainly hadn't seen any fairy folk there, or anywhere else for that matter. That was, until the day he was sent to cut peat for Farmer Brown.

Wullie had cut a good swathe of thick turf from the side of Merlin's Crag, stacked it carefully in Brown's cart, and was about to take the load back down the track to the byre, when he was startled by the sudden appearance of a tiny woman, about the size of a small child, right before him. She looked very annoyed.

Waving her hand in front of Wullie's face, she yelled, 'You stop right there, William Hannah, for those are my turfs you're stealing.'

She pointed a tiny finger at the freshly dug hillside, and stamped her petite foot in frustration.

'See what you've done to the roof of my hoose? How would you like it if I were to remove the thatch roof that covers your cottage? What would your wife and bairns say to you then, when the rain and wind blew in?!'

Wullie was speechless. All he could do was make a surprised stuttering sound, as he stared dumbfounded at the little fairy woman. For he realised right away that this was what she must be. The local people often spoke about the Crag belonging to the 'Wee Folk', and here was the tiniest, yet most perfectly formed, woman he had ever seen. Her dress and shawl were woven in many shades of green, which shimmered and sparkled in the sunlight. When she stamped her foot in indignation at Wullie, he glimpsed a flash of her berry-red stockings and a pair of dainty leather boots. He marvelled at her bonnie, elfin features and golden hair, which hung in wild loose curls around her shoulders. Wullie thought that she was the most beautiful creature he had ever seen.

Her sharp voice brought him back to his senses.

'Now, you put those peats right back exactly where you took them from, or I will be vexed.'

Wullie did as he was told, replacing the turfs immediately. He knew that if anyone upset the fairy folk, they could be very spiteful in return. He did not want to risk offending the fairy any further in case she took revenge on him or his family. After all, she knew his name, so she probably knew where he lived too!

He laid each turf back where he had taken it from, and stamped them carefully into place. When he had finished the work he felt exhausted but he took the time to check over the peats, making sure that they fitted snugly together. Satisfied he'd done a good job, he turned back to see if the fairy woman approved, but she had vanished.

Wullie led the horse and cart back to the farm and explained to Farmer Brown why, after he had spent the whole day labouring on the hillside, he had returned without any peat.

'Perhaps I should go to the other side of the moor tomorrow sir and fetch you peats from an ordinary place, wi none of these fairy folk to hinder me,' he suggested enthusiastically.

Farmer Brown listened in amazement to Wullie's story. But he was a modern man, who believed in science, not old fairy stories and superstitions. With a scowl and the threat of, 'No pay', he sent Wullie right back out with the horse and cart to Merlin's Crag. He demanded that Wullie put the peats back in the cart, then bring them to the barn to dry out that same evening.

Wullie set off, once again, along the bumpy, winding hill track, until he reached Merlin's Crag and the place where he had cut and returned the blocks of peat earlier that day. He pulled the turfs back up and, keeping his eyes down, he threw the peats into the cart. Making the sign of the cross before he left the hillside, Wullie prayed that no curse would follow him home, and that his work for the farmer would be forgiven by the wee people.

As days rolled into weeks and many months went past without any ill luck befalling Wullie, he began to relax and think perhaps he had just imagined his meeting with the little woman. It was probably just a vivid dream, which he had confused in his mind with real life. Summer, autumn and winter all went by without incident and as a new spring approached Wullie Hannah had completely forgotten about his strange encounter with the fairy.

However, exactly one year later, Wullie was working for Farmer Brown again, chopping a fallen tree into firewood. Happy with the well-stacked log pile, the farmer paid Wull his due and also gave him a can of fresh cow's milk to take home to his wife.

Pleased with the extra bonus, Wullie set off for home at dusk, taking the winding track up and over the hills. As he reached the very spot at Merlin's Crag where he had been digging peat a year ago, he paused and yawned. His eyelids felt heavy and a sudden exhaustion came over him, upon which he sank down to rest on a tuft of grass. Perhaps a quick nap would help him overcome this tiredness, he thought, before closing his eyes and sinking into a sound sleep.

When he awoke Wullie felt groggy, and as his senses came back he realised that he was still lying on the hillside, only now he was surrounded by little people. The fairies were dancing all around him in a flurry of laughter and music. Some were waving their little fists and fingers in his face. The moon lit up the scene, as fairy fiddlers and pipers played faster tunes and the dancers turned and whirled more wildly around the big man.

'Dance wi us Wullie,' called elfin voices, all echoing in time to the hypnotic rhythm of the strange music.

Never in his life had Wullie felt comfortable getting up to dance – 'two-left feet', was his excuse for staying seated on village ceilidh nights. But now the fairy folk were pulling him to his feet and pushing him into the middle of their circle. A fairy lass sprang to his side and pulled him around by his hands. As she tugged him one way and then the other, he began to feel an electricity throughout his entire being, and he leapt around the grassy dance floor like a frisky hare, or a bird on the wing. All night he span, pranced and flourished, as if he were a ballet dancer.

When the first farm cockerel crowed its morning tune, the host of fairies ended their merry party on the hillside and flocked towards the rocks, at the height of Merlin's Crag. They pulled Wull along with them. As they reached the first boulder, a chasm appeared between the rocks and the horde of little fairy men and women disappeared deep underground, dragging Wullie far beneath the hill.

Wullie's legs ached from all the dancing, and he collapsed on to a flat rock at the edge of the subterranean cave. He watched the wee folk fall into pillows of gossamer- and fleece-covered couches, dotted about the dimly lit cavern. All of them fell into deep sleep, with radiant, peaceful smiles upon their tiny faces.

After a very sound sleep, Wullie awoke. He was still on the rock floor, deep underground in the fairy's realm. The wee people were waking too and going about their business. The man sat quietly watching in complete wonder, as the little creatures did the most strange and unusual things. Many of their occupations were so unexpected and new to Wullie, that his mouth hung open in awe – these fairy industries involved training mice, decorating beetles, massaging worms, tickling woodlice's tummies, and many other different types of botanical alchemy and nature crafts that were far beyond Wullie's, or any mortal's ken (understanding)!

When the long day of diligent and supernatural fairy toil was finished, an elfin woman approached Wullie. He recognised her instantly, it was the golden-haired fairy with the red stockings who had told him to put the turf back on her roof, a year ago.

'Well man, I'm satisfied. That's my roof grown back, and the rain is no longer seeping into my house. You've paid your dues and now you can go home, a free man. But Willie Hannah, you must swear an oath, never to tell anyone what you have seen here, in our fairy halls.'

Wullie promised faithfully never to share the fairy's secret crafts with his own humankind, and then she took his hand and led him back to the entrance, high in the rocks above. Wullie stumbled out into the bright warm, light of the sun.

The first thing he noticed was the can of milk that Farmer Brown had given to him. It was sitting on a rock, just where he had left it – still fresh – his wife would be delighted with that, even though he might have a hard job explaining to her where he had been all night! Wullie sprinted back down the hill to his wee house, and barged in noisily. He hung up his hat and coat and put the milk can down on the table.

'I'm back my dearies, and what a tale I've got to tell!' he called out merrily to his family. But as he turned and saw his wife, coming in through the door, he saw her face drain of colour, and she sank down on to the tiled floor. He ran to help her up and sat her down in a chair.

'Whatever is wrong my dear, are you sick? Why, you look like you've seen a ghost!' He lifted a pitcher from the counter and poured her a cup of water.

When she was recovered enough to speak, she shook her head in disbelief and through bitter tears asked him why he had been so cruel to leave them for so long?

It wasn't until his five children walked into the room that he realised what she meant. When he had seen them last, they had been only wee tots, the eldest seven years old, and now they were much bigger, his son a teenager, almost a man, and the others all many years older.

Finally, Wullie Hannah managed to figure it all out; that one day in the land of the fairy folk had been seven years in the mortal world. He had indeed paid the price for damaging a fairy's roof! From then on, when Wullie was sent to cut peat for the fire, he took it from the other side of the Lanarkshire moors. He preferred to walk an extra mile, out of his way, to avoid walking over Merlin's Crag, and he never encountered the fairies ever again.

6

THE OLDEST MAN IN SCOTLAND

Leadhills is the second highest village in Scotland, standing at 395m (1,295ft) above sea level. Surrounded by the beautiful curves of the Lowther Hills, which form part of the Southern Uplands Way, it is the southernmost boundary of South Lanarkshire. The village was once a thriving silver, gold and lead-mining community. Records show that these precious metals were being excavated here as far back as Roman times, if not before. In the 1500s, gold from Leadhills was used to make crowns for James V and his Queen, and most of the coins during his and Mary Queen of Scots' reigns were minted from gold mined from the area. It was once known as 'God's treasure-house in Scotland'. Now the village is a stop-off point for hill walkers, who eat and stay at the Hopetoun Arms Hotel, nestled among the rows of old miners' cottages. During the summer months you can visit the Leadhills Miners' Library, the oldest subscription library in Britain, which contains many rare books and a collection of local minerals. However, Leadhills has another exceptional claim besides its elevated golf course, precious metals and mesmerising scenery, and that is the gravestone of John Taylor, who just happened to have been the oldest man in Scotland. Within the graveyard is an old headstone inscribed with the words, 'John Taylor, Miner, aged 137'.

John Taylor was the son of a miner from Aldstone, Cumberland. He was probably born in 1637 and died in 1770, making him 133 years old when he died, and not the fabled 137 years inscribed on his gravestone. We can forgive the headstone engraver and John's grieving family for miscalculating his age by four years because John still wins the title of the Oldest Man in Scotland.

In an era when many people's ages were not officially recorded, it was not uncommon for folk to not know their exact age.

His actual year of birth was eventually calculated by his family, and local historians, because of a significant celestial event and the time in history when children were allowed to work underground, in mines. John's father died when he was only four years old, leaving the family to cope with extreme poverty. This left his mother with no choice other than to work down the mines and take the children with her – they all worked for the mining company. Wee toddler John had to wash ore by hand for two pence a day. On the day of the celebrated total eclipse of the sun, in 1652, young John was at the bottom of Winlock shaft, where he had been working as a kibble boy for at least three or four years. John would recount that on the day called 'Mirk Monday' Thomas Millbank called down the pit shaft for him to, 'Tell the men below to come up and behold the wonder, for a curious cloud has darkened the sun, and the birds are falling to earth.'

The miners put down their tools and went up to marvel at the rare, astronomical event, many of whom had never seen anything like it before in their lives, including John, who was now aged about fifteen. The eclipse left an unparalleled and lasting impression on all who saw it that day.

John laboured hard in mines most of his life. He married a lass that he met on the island of Islay, and they lived happily together, raising a family of nine children. They moved around the mining districts of Northern England and Scotland, until coming to Leadhills with their family in 1733. Here, they settled peacefully in their retirement. John had survived scurvy, which he had suffered from after the poor diet he was fed of salt-meat and whisky when working in the lead mines at Strontian, Argyll. He survived almost bleeding to death when a negligent surgeon had bled him for a fever, and left the wound to bleed until blood soaked through the ceiling on to the heads of his family in the room below. He also lived to tell the tale of when, at the age of 100, his nearest and dearest left him outside the cottage for a night, 'in case God had forgotten him'.

Another local story from John's life is told of how when he was a 116 years of age, one day in late September, he set out over the hills to go fishing. While following two burns upstream to catch trout, unexpectedly, he was caught on all sides by a fierce snow blizzard. He stuck his rod upright in the snow and struggled through the thick drifts, but the ferocity of the blizzard left him unable to find his way back home. Fortunately, when he did not return in time for dinner, his family rang the curfew bell and organised a rescue party. The rescuers battled through the snowstorm and were lucky enough to find him alive. They carried him safely home to his cottage at Gold Scars, where a warm hearth and dinner awaited him. A few days later, when the weather had improved, John set off back into the hills to retrieve his fishing rod!

His wife died in 1758, after forty-nine years of married life with John, who would have been 106 years old when she died.

He was described as, 'A thin, spare man of 5ft 8in, black-haired, ruddy faced, and long-visaged, who always had a good appetite.'

Maybe it was John's 'good appetite', for a breakfast of porridge, broth, meat and 'malt liquor', the fresh, clean air of the Southern Uplands and his family's love for him. Whatever the magical elixir was that kept him alive for so long, he lived for another twelve years after his wife's death. Aged 128 years, John was still able to walk uphill 2 miles from his cottage into the village to entertain his grandchildren at the Ale House, then walk 2 miles home again. His family must have known how lucky they were to have such a special father and grandfather, and the gravestone they erected in his memory, at the cemetery in Leadhills, is testament to their love and respect for John Taylor, the 'Oldest Man in Scotland'.

7

FAIRY TALES
FROM DOUGLAS

*These two stories from Douglas Dale are about living in harmony
with the fairy folk. They are ascribed to the 'Dear Years' in Scotland,
which were in the first half of the eighteenth century. This was a time
when harvests failed due to poor weather conditions and famine followed – because wheat, oats and barley seeds were too dear for most
farmers to buy during this time, it led to the planting of a new, rela-
tively unknown crop, which could survive the harsher weather – the
potato! The belief in fairy or nature spirits as guardians of the natural
world was perhaps a remnant of the pagan past, but it was clearly still
prevalent amongst the rural communities of Scotland in the 1700s.
Whether you are a believer in the existence of fairies, or not, their folk
stories gifted to us from the country people of years gone by serve as a
kindly reminder to treat the non-human world with kindness and
respect and reap your just rewards!*

Bert Bruce had been farming all his days. After his parents'
passing, he inherited the small farm in Douglas Parish. The
solid, single-storey farmhouse was comfortable enough for Bert
and the two good-sized fields gave him plenty of work and a
very tidy profit from the annual harvests. He had come late to
love and at the time of this tale, aged thirty-two, Bert had just

begun dating Lizzie Prentice, a local seamstress from Douglas village. They'd met at the summer Gala Day and enjoyed each other's company so much that they began to sit next to each other at the kirk services every Sunday, followed by a stroll through the parish and lunch together. After a few weeks, Bert had plucked up the courage to ask for Lizzie's hand in marriage and, delighted at her acceptance, he paid a deposit on a gold ring for his darling wife-to-be from the goldsmith in Lanark. Everything was working out well for Bert and Lizzie, until the dreadful harvest of that year, 1742.

Bert and his sweetheart had hardly noticed the awful, wet weather that summer, as they only had eyes for each other – seeing the world through the rose-tinted hue of new love. But when the time arrived to bring in the oats, barley and wheat, Bert was shocked to find his fields and crops had been smitten with fungus and disease, which had thrived in the unseasonal wet weather conditions. With the corn ruined, Bert made no profit from farming that year. Lizzie agreed with Bert that they should wait until the following year to marry, and their wedding was postponed.

After a winter of further harsh weather, which continued stormily well into spring, all of Scotland's farming communities were struck with poverty and the entire country with famine.

Bert had always worked diligently on his land: tending the fertility of the soil, weeding carefully, harvesting gently, so that mice and rabbits could escape the cut of the scythe, and leaving the trees in his shelter belt to grow and thrive, creating a safe haven for all of the wild creatures and plants that he shared the land with. His efforts were usually rewarded with fine harvests, which kept him financially buoyant. After the failed crop of the previous year, Bert had nothing to sow that spring and was forced to travel to Biggar to buy overpriced seeds from a grain merchant. The prices were the dearest they had ever been and in such short supply and high demand that Bert had to spend all of his savings to buy one very small bagful of oats and barley. He plodded home to Douglas that afternoon with a light bag of grain and a very heavy heart. Along the way, he watched destitute people, scavenging in barren fields for the leaves of peas and beans, while other desperate folk wandered the woodlands and verges, eating sorrel and other wild plants. Poor folk were starving to death. And succumbing to all the diseases of the times.

The next morning, Bert was up with the sunrise and he took the meagre bag of oat and barley seed to his fields, which he had ploughed, ready for planting. Storm clouds rolled across the sun and a bitter wind blew relentlessly from the north. Bert walked up and down row after row of neatly furrowed soil, stooping to

press the few precious seeds into the earth. His future and a life of love and partnership with Lizzie depended entirely on the success of this crop.

When he had planted every seed, Bert stood tall, stretching his back and legs, as he surveyed the ground he had covered. Rain had come on, driven by the wind, horizontally slashing into his face. He groaned in despair, as he saw that less than one third of his field was planted. He looked into his seed sack, hoping to find one or two more seeds, but it was empty. So was Bert's soul, empty of any hope of surviving the famine to come, or of marrying his sweet Lizzie. He dropped to his knees in the wet, bare dirt and sobbed.

He hadn't let the tears of anguish flood from his eyes for long, when Bert heard a voice calling out from the thorn bushes behind him. He caught his breath, stopped crying and turned to see who had spoken. He saw no one, but then the voice called again clearly, 'Tak – an' gie, as guid to me.'

Bert couldn't see the speaker, but between a hawthorn and blackthorn, he spotted a large sack full of something. He didn't know what to do and stood gawping at the invisible stranger's sack. The voice called for a third time, but addressed him directly, 'Bert Bruce, do you ken the sack?'

Bert nodded in agreement to the bushes.

'Well man, heed ma words – Tak – an gie, as guid to me!'

A peel of laughter trilled out of the thicket, then disappeared in the wind.

Bert approached the sack cautiously. When he opened it up and peered inside, there were the freshest, healthiest-looking oat seeds he had ever seen in his life, and the sack was filled full with this rich commodity. After mumbling 'thank you kindly' to the empty thorn trees, he set right back to work, walking up and down the land, sowing the gifted oats. By the end of the day, both his fields were fully planted. With an aching back but glad heart, Bert retired to his home and slept soundly, dreaming of golden corn fields and happy scenes of family life with Lizzie.

Despite more bad weather, Bert's oat crop thrived, growing strong and luxuriant. The harvest was equally bountiful. Bert had never grown such an abundance of fine grain before, and he reaped the benefit financially at the harvest market. He had carefully preserved the sack the oat seed had come in, and as soon as the crop was ready, he filled it back up to the top with the very best of the fairy oats – well, that's what Lizzie had said about the lucky oat sack; 'It must be the work of a kindly fairy!' Bert took this to the exact spot he had found it in and placed it down next to the bushes. He hadn't waited long when a voice called to him, 'Turn roun' your back, while I get my sack.'

The farmer averted his face, but curiosity immediately got the better of him and he turned round quickly to look. There was nothing there, all had vanished!

Bert and Lizzie's wedding was the grandest in the county and alms and grain were given to all of the poor people in Douglas by the generous couple. Their farm prospered from that day on, and they raised their family to respect the fairy folk, always leaving a gift of grain at harvest time in the thorn bushes, at the edge of the fields, which were left wild and natural for the wee folk to dwell in.

NB: In the original source, there is a poem ascribed to this tale:

> Meddle an' mell'
> Wi' the fien's o' hell,
> An a werdless wicht ye'll be;
> But tak an' len',
> Wi' the fairy men,
> Ye'll thrive ay while ye dee.

(In the *Scottish Journal of Topography*, 1847, p.150).

8

NANNIE'S
INVISIBLE HELPER

During the terrible years of famine in Scotland in the 1740s, an old woman from Douglas Parish ran out of food. After one day without anything to eat, she went to bed early to try and sleep through the hunger. When she awoke the next morning, she was greatly surprised to find that her linen bonnet, which hung over the bedpost, was completely full of fine oatmeal. 'What a delightful present,' thought old Nannie, and she took it straight to her cooking pan and made herself a large bowl of porridge for breakfast. As she felt her strength returning, Nannie visited each of her neighbours in turn, to find out who had filled her cap with meal and saved her from starvation. But all of them denied leaving the gift of grain. Less friendly folk took offence, angry at Nannie's inquiry, replying rudely, 'We have little enough to feed our own bairns, let alone an old biddy like you!' After this, Nannie certainly knew better who liked her in the village, and who didn't, but she was no closer to knowing who had been kind enough to gift her the oats.

Every morning, Nannie used only a tiny measure of oats for her breakfast porridge. Then she would scrape the cooking pan, using the glutinous, oaty residue to make a stock with water and herbs. This she heated into a thin soup, which sufficed Nannie for dinner and supper and staved off her hunger. One morning, she traded a cup of her precious oatmeal for a duck egg from a farmer's wife. She boiled the egg and chopped it up together with leaves from a hawthorn bush, bittercress from the garden and hedge mustard, which grew wild along the lane. This meagre dish lasted her for three days. Nannie was scrupulously careful and thrifty with the oatmeal, eking out her rations for as long as possible, but eventually the meal was all used up. Once more, the fear of starvation filled the old woman with dread and her stomach grumbled and growled with hunger for a day and a night. She visited all of her neighbours again, explaining that she had no food left, and asking for any spare kitchen scraps, but no one had anything to give. Nannie went to bed with an empty stomach and troubled mind.

She woke the next morning, and to her surprise and delight, her bonnet – still hanging from the bedpost – was again filled to the brim with high-quality oatmeal. She ran to the door and poked her head out, scanning the lane for whoever might have sneaked into her home and left the life-saving grain. She saw a fox trotting across a field and birds singing noisily in the hedges, but there was no sign of people in Douglas so early in the morning. Nannie cooked and ate a bigger bowl of porridge than was usual, to satisfy her empty stomach. Soon, she felt her vitality return, and Nannie went to visit her friends in the village, to see if any would confess to leaving the gift in her bonnet. Once again, every-one denied knowing anything about the oatmeal, and several of them begged her to give them a little of the mystery grain. Nannie did what she could for her hungry friends, but times were so exceptionally difficult for poor folk that she kept most of the oats for herself. This time, Nannie was even more frugal with her grain, and she walked many miles each day to forage for herbs and berries in the hedges, woodlands and fields of the parish. Anything she found was either eaten immediately or put in a little cloth bag and taken home. Roots and nuts she ground up to mix in with the oats, and this meal was patted into bannocks and cooked on the griddle, while she used nettles, herbs and berries to add flavour to thin gruels and soups. Nannie's ingenuity with what little food she had was exceptional and she made the second cap-full of oats last even longer than the first. But inevitably, they were all used up!

Again, Nannie spent a day and a night with nothing to eat and hunger pangs tormented her terribly. The first thing she did on waking, on this occasion, was to check her hanging bonnet for meal, and to her relief, it was once more filled to the brim with good oatmeal. Nannie knelt beside her bed and wept for joy, then she whispered a little prayer of thanks, to whoever her mystery benefactor might be. Ever resourceful with her valuable food source, Nannie made the oatmeal last longer than before. But when it was finished and she had suffered a day and night without food, the bonnet was, once more, mysteriously replenished. This pattern continued repeatedly, for many months, until Nannie was well fed, secure and healthy.

Now, taking her magical supply of meal for granted, she decided to invite her friends and neighbours around for a meal. Nannie offered the butcher some of her best herb oaten cakes in return for a cut of meat, which she cooked in a stew, with angelica root and peas. Using up the entire bonnet-full of oatmeal, she made another batch of extra deep oat cakes. Her guests arrived and were amazed by the lavish spread of good food awaiting them on Old Nan's table. When everyone was seated and ready to begin the meal, Nannie banged her spoon on a kettle, to silence the chattering crowd. She smiled warmly – and perhaps a little smugly – at her dinner guests and began to make a speech of thanks, followed by a request for bowed heads and eyes, while they joined in with a prayer of thanks. When Nannie had finished thanking the Lord for his bounteous gifts, she opened her eyes and cried, 'Let's eat!' As the guests enthusiastically began to reach for their plates, a sudden gust

of wind wooshed down the chimney and blew the door open.
The neighbours watched, incredulous, as all of the oaten cakes
rose up from the table of their own accord, hovered in the air
for a moment and then flipped over and landed back on the
table. The dinner guests were startled to see that all of the cakes
had changed into withered-up stalks of kale. Nannie's friends
rubbed their eyes in astonishment at this supernatural sight,
but then everyone jumped in fright as a voice thundered from
out of nowhere:

> Never mair
> O' mine ye's share,
> But want an wae
> Till your deein' day!

The guests fled from the house as fast as possible, leaving any
thought of stew, cakes … or kale behind.

Sadly, Nannie didn't recover from
this terrifying experience. Her
bonnet was never filled
with oatmeal by her
invisible helper again,
who was clearly
offended by Nannie's
attempt to share the
gift, and she ended
her days as a deaf,
old soul, driven by
poverty to beg for
food from door to door.

9

THE LEGEND OF CORA LINN

Close to the World Heritage mill village of New Lanark are the magnificent waterfalls at Cora Lynn, or Linn (Linn is Gaelic for pool). This is the biggest waterfall (by volume of water) in the UK, but one rarely sees it in full spate due to the weir upstream, which diverts water for the hydroelectric scheme. On the Corehouse Estate side of the river, above the falls, are the ruins of Cora Castle – built for the Bannatyne family in the fifteenth century. The walk from New Lanark to the castle is glorious – the paths, which were originally created by Lady Mary Ross from the Bonnington Estate during the Victorian era for early tourism, are well maintained by the Scottish Wildlife Trust, the surrounding landscape being a dedicated National Wildlife Reserve.

A legend was popular during the nineteenth century that the falls and castle were named after King Malcolm II's daughter, Cora. However, a short version of this tale told in History of Lanark, *1835, ends by letting the reader know that 'Cora' comes from the Gaelic word 'currach', meaning marshy, therefore the tale is purely fiction.*

The story that follows takes its inspiration from another, romantic Victorian version of the tale, printed in Graham's Illustrated Magazine, *in 1856.*

Many centuries ago, Malcolm II of Scotland lived with his beautiful daughter Cora in one of the country's most stunning locations. Their castle was perched high on a cliff edge, in Lanarkshire, above the waterfall now known as the Falls of Clyde. In local tradition, the falls are called Cora Linn and the once proud stronghold, Cora Castle. This is the legend of how they acquired their name.

King Malcolm was known to be a wise and peaceful king. While he reigned on the throne of Scotland, the common folk had plenty of work on the land, and the marketplaces were thriving with goods and life. The merchants and traders grew rich from mastering the seas and selling their bounty. Everyone in the country was happy and well fed.

Princess Cora was the youngest of Malcolm's daughters. Although the King tried not to show favouritism, he couldn't help but adore his youngest girl, and allowed her anything she wanted. Cora reminded the King so much of her mother, who sadly had died and now lay in a tomb on Iona. Her sisters were all married to rich and powerful thanes and lords of Scotland, leaving only Cora at home with her father. She was renowned for her natural beauty, which had the effect of attracting unmarried nobleman from all of Britain and Ireland, and from faraway lands as well. Her father particularly approved of three of these potential suitors – Kenneth, a Lord of the Isles; Graeme, Thane of Strathearn; and Dunbar, Thane of Lothian. They were sons of his allies and men of important influence in the kingdom. He was particularly keen for her to marry one of these worthy nobles, and was happy to let her choose the one she liked best.

Cora'a beauty was startling, just as her mother's had been. A radiant complexion, clear, kind eyes and a shock of thick, wavy, nut-brown hair, which she insisted on keeping short. Although cropped hair was rather an unusual style for a lady of her rank, it suited her natural high spirits and sporting charm. For Cora loved more than anything to ride and hunt in the kingdom's verdant forests.

Her horse, a fine-boned, hot-blooded Arabian mare, gifted to her by Gregory Bishop of St Andrews, was quite unlike any of the local breeds, which looked like poor plough nags in comparison. A silver bridle with thirteen silver bells had been presented to her along with the mare. Cora delighted in awarding the bells as trophies to the winners of horse races held at nearby Lanark Racecourse. Horsemen on magnificent steeds came from all over the county to take part in Cora's Silver Bell Royal Races. Many of the competitors, however, were far more interested in winning the princess's attention than the precious silver bells.

At home, Cora's father made sure she was lavished with everything possible to keep his lass contented. Her bedchamber was hung with glittering, oriental silks and colourful tapestries to brighten the stone walls. The windows were glazed with cut, polished beryl and the floors carpeted with sheepskin and furs, the most luxurious draught-proofing money could buy. When harsh winter weather prevented her from hunting, she was content to stay in by the fire and play harp, singing for the King and their household. The three suitors were each invited regularly, but separately, to attend these cosy ceilidhs by her father. Cora, however, never showed much interest in any of them.

Her father tried to remain patient – after all, it would take time to choose between such incredibly fine young men. He recognised the unique and valuable assets that each of these potential husbands possessed. Months rolled into years and by Cora's twenty-third birthday, Malcolm knew that his patience with her was running out!

In a final attempt to ignite a love match between his daughter and one of the Scottish lords, King Malcolm organised a fine party to celebrate the princess's birthday. Kenneth, Graeme and Dunbar were invited, as well as a few extra eligible bachelors. After feasting, toasting, speeches and cake, the guests were invited to dance in the great hall. Musicians played and singers warbled old and modern melodies. Intoxicated guests grew loud and boisterous, and castle dogs were banished to the courtyard after paws had been trodden on by enthusiastic dancers. At the height of the amusement, Cora made an excuse to take her favourite dog away from the rumbustious crowd and quietly exited the celebration. When she had not returned after some time and many of the revellers were too tired or drunk to continue partying, King Malcolm, in need of fresh air, took his leave of the gathering and slipped away to walk through the woods, clear his head and look for his missing daughter.

Enjoying the soothing sound of bird call, a relieving tonic after the clamour and noise of the birthday party, the King strolled down a pine-needle-carpeted slope towards the burn. This was his special place, where he could enjoy his own company, relax and rest awhile. He often came here to contemplate matters in peace, away from the bustle of castle life. Rounding the curve of the hillside, he stopped in his tracks, baffled by what he saw ahead of him. It appeared that someone else knew of this secluded spot, hidden deep in his royal forest. For down below on the bridge were a man and woman, wrapped together in a passionate embrace. Malcolm watched silently from his vantage point, unsure whether to turn quietly away and leave the lovers to their affair or go on to his intended sanctuary and chase the couple off his land. Before he could make up his mind, a strange sensation took hold of him. A realisation of familiarity began to paralyse his soul. The woman's mantle of yellow linen, a tunic of scarlet silk, shoulder-length bronze curls, like a page boy's. Malcolm's eyes darted to the man; a linked mail vest, steel cap with eagle wings emblem, bow and quiver, boar spear, belt with knife and silver bugle. It was his head huntsmen, Ian MacDhu, son of Red John, and the woman he was kissing was his own daughter, Cora!

In a fury, King Malcolm stumbled down the hill towards the lovers. His anger was so blinding that, senseless with rage, he pulled out his knife and pressed it into the huntsman's chest.

MacDhu fell to his knees before the King, offering no resistance. The cries of his daughter and her frenzied grip on his arm brought Malcolm back to consciousness. He drew breath and paused, the knife in his hand was piercing the traitor's skin. Cora was face down on the earth, clinging to his legs and wailing hysterically for him to stop. It was MacDhu's deep, soft voice that brought the King back to a state of reason. He was offering his life to Malcolm, and begging him to forgive his child and blame only him, Iain MacDhu. Cora wept and wailed, 'I love only him, take my life if you must kill anyone.'

The sight of her precious face, covered in dirt from the ground, and her beautiful birthday robes, torn and stained, made Malcolm stop and draw back the knife. MacDhu was the best huntsman he had ever know, better than the father, Red John, who had served him loyally his entire life. The King decided in an instant to spare the foolish man's life.

'I will spare you Iain MacDhu, but only because of my respect for your father, who was a faithful servant. You will, however, leave my sight and my lands immediately. If you are found anywhere within thirty miles of my castle, after three days, I will have you torn to pieces, tied to ropes between wild horses. Never show your face here again, and you must never look on my daughter's. Leave!'

MacDhu staggered to his feet, his eyes filled with tears, and went without another word. King Malcolm pulled Cora up from the forest path and marched his disgraced girl back to the castle. She was hurriedly bustled past the remaining birthday guests and locked in her bedchamber.

Two days later, Malcolm had decided that the best thing that could be done with his wilful daughter was to take her to the Black Abbess of Iona. Here he knew that prayer, fasting and the Abbess's reputation for being stern would mend Cora's headstrong impudence.

Meanwhile, with word spreading fast that MacDhu was no longer looking after the King's forest, poachers were arriving, scouring the wild habitats unchallenged, killing whatever creatures they liked.

Not wanting to waste any more time, the King had his daughter and servants packed by sunrise, ready to escort her to Iona himself. They had gone only a short distance from the castle and were trekking steadily over the rocky ground above the great waterfall, when a clear sharp blast from a hunting bugle pierced the air. All of the horses startled at the noise, but Cora's Arab mare took fright and bolted from the group. As the horse galloped out of control along the path, another high note from the hunting horn echoed around the river gorge and the terrified beast stumbled, slipped and fell towards the cliff edge. Cora screamed as her horse skidded over the precipice, tumbling down into the foaming torrent of water below. The King's party looked in vain for woman and horse in the tumult of surging water, but nothing of them could be seen. The body of the mare was found three days later, downstream at the village of Kirkholme. Cora's was not, she was believed to be lost forever. King Malcolm retired to his apartments to grieve for his lost child. From that time, the castle and waterfall became known as Cora Castle and Cora Linn, in memory of the King's youngest daughter.

What became of Iain MacDhu? Well, on that fateful day when Cora fell into the River Clyde, it was his hunting horn that had frightened the horses. He had hidden downstream of the waterfall, and as the King escorted Cora from the castle, Iain had blown his horn and watched as her highly strung horse panicked and plummeted with Cora into the falls. He leaped into the water, unseen from the riverbank, and pulled his love to safety. Shaken and bruised, she survived the ordeal virtually unscathed. Sadly, the beautiful mare was swept away by the strong currents before Iain could grab the reins and rescue her. Together the couple escaped along the embankment, under cover of trees and bushes. At Cadzow, Iain had arranged to meet a monk in his cave cell. Here, in the Avon Gorge, the lovers were married. Travelling mostly at night, they made their escape undetected by the King and his retinue. Eventually they settled in the Highlands, in the Forest of Glen Fiddich, where they lived peacefully in a modest stone cottage. Iain made a living from hunting and Cora learned to weave, taught by kindly local women. Soon children were born to the young couple, and their family thrived together, in a loving household.

And what of King Malcolm II of Scotland? Malcolm grew grey with age and grief. Eight years after his daughter's fall into the waters of the Clyde, in the year 1009, Malcolm was forced into war with the Danes. His army marched north and a great battle ensued. During the brutal fighting, the King was on the point of being slaughtered by two Danish commanders, when a tall, brawny man appeared, dispatched the Danes, and saved King Malcolm. The loyal Highlander, who had appeared just at the right moment to rescue the monarch from certain death, disappeared just as quickly and mysteriously. With no time to ponder the miraculous occurrence, Malcolm made his way from the battlefield, heading towards the shelter of the forest. He stopped at a burn to refresh himself, cleaning blood and dirt from face and hands. As he drew water and drank from the burn, he spoke with a local child who was filling her bucket from the clear cold current. The little girl had curly brown hair and a pretty face that reminded the old king of someone he had known. The King was battle weary and weak, so the child led him to her mother and father's croft in the woods. Here King Malcolm was reunited with his youngest daughter, Cora, and the many grandchildren he had never known. When the tall fighter who had killed the Danes appeared in the doorway of the humble little cottage and his children ran to hug him, Malcolm knew full well Iain MacDhu's loyalty and worth. Cora tended to her husband's and father's battle wounds while the children prepared food. Stories were told and tears of joy shed during their meal together. They sat, long into the night, sharing their adventures and rekindling the flame of love and kinship. Naturally the King forgave Iain and Cora's past wrongdoing, and gave their marriage and children his blessing. Eventually, the reunited family returned to their castle and lands in the Clyde Valley, and lived happily till the end of their royal days.

10

STORIES AND FOLKLORE FROM LANARK'S CASTLEGATE

Nestling in the very centre of the county of Lanarkshire is the Royal Burgh of Lanark. It's from this small, southern market town of Lanark that the whole county takes its name. Historians believe that there has been a settlement here since at least 6500 BCE. The archaeologists' finds of arrowheads and fragments of pottery, discovered at the old Lanark auction site, belonged to the Mesolithic people of this distant past.

Saint Kentigern's Church, now a preserved ruin, probably dates back to the founding of the Royal Burgh of Lanark, by David I, around 1140–1150. Both this church and Lanark's Saint Nicholas's Church were owned by the monks of Dryburgh Abbey (also now a preserved ruin, near Melrose). St Nicholas's was first recorded in 1214, when a gift of candles was made. It has undergone renovation since then, including moving the entrance from the west to the east side of the building. Sculptor Robert Forest's impressive statue of William Wallace (1822) looks out proudly from above the church doors. A historical hero of Scottish independence, his fixed stone eyes perpetually watch Lanark High Street. This part of Lanark is known as Castlegate. Across from Wallace's statue there is an unimposing gap among the row of buildings. This is where a medieval townhouse once stood, belonging to Marion Braidfute, and where William Wallace lived briefly with his wife and daughter (there is a plaque marking the spot). Here in this humble, grey, gap site, Wallace's most dramatic fight for freedom began. This is the story of Wallace and Marion in Lanark.

WILLIAM WALLACE AND MARION BRAIDFUTE

After Wallace and his friends had ambushed English troops at Loudon Hill, their success gave them the appetite to continue to wage an uprising against the occupation of Scotland by Edward I's men. It was winter 1296 and this small band of freedom fighters knew it was time to hunker down and gather their forces for greater battles and bigger fights in the coming year. William settled down to enjoy the comforts of his uncle's home at Kilbank, in the parish of Lesmahagow. Some of his compatriots also had family around the Douglas and Clydesdale district, and a couple lodged near William and his uncle's family. The members of the resistance band met regularly at Saint Kentigern's Church for Sunday service, in the town of Lanark. It was just a couple of miles from Wallace's lodgings and as he and his friends made their way along the dirt roads into Lanark, it became easy sport for them to dispatch any English soldiers they met along the way. The news of these murders spread fast across the district, frightening English sheriffs and their military henchmen, while the Scots folk, who hated their oppressors, were secretly delighted.

On Christmas Day the ancient Church of St Kentigern's was filled with the good and the worthy of the parish. The pews were full and the aisles and naves were jammed with ordinary folk, kneeling or standing while older, less able souls leaned on relatives for support. The bitter winter sleet and rain blew hard against windows and through cracks in doors, causing the candles to flicker and splutter. The Mass was lit by over a hundred tallow candles, which gave the church an aura of sanctity and Christian warmth. The gathered crowd, moved by the priest's tale of the birth of the Christ child and the hope for the world through the salvation of Christ, forgot, even if just for a few moments, their worries and cares. William Wallace and the men who fought with him against the English occupation of their homeland felt the holy message as if it were a personal mantra for their cause – Christ's birth and presence, there to free them from enslavement and tyranny; Christ's story echoing their spiritual right, to be free from the corrupt and evil occupation of Edward I's army. As William cast his eyes casually about the throng of worshippers, noting any Englishmen, or strangers to the town, he noticed a young noble woman, sitting towards the front of the chapel. Her mantle was that of the titled class, but what caught William's attention was her beautiful face.

Marion Braidfute sat in St Kentigern's Church, barely able to hear the Christmas Mass on that cold winter's day. Instead, her mind was gripped in turmoil at the painful memory of losing both her father and her mother in recent times and now, just in the past few days, her own dear brother. Marion's heart and mind were crippled by sadness and pain.

The priest's words droned on before her, but she found little comfort in their meaning, as the message of Christ could not be felt in a community surrounded by vengeful, barbaric and murderous overlords. Hugh de Braidfute, Marion's brother, had come to live with her in her father's Lanark townhouse in order to keep away from the troops ransacking the houses of the noble Scottish families. But Heselrig, the Sheriff of Lanark appointed by King Edward, the English fiend, had sought her sibling out and murdered him in the doorway of their own house for no other reason than that he was a Scotsman. As Marion's mind played over the horrendous events of her brother's death, a tear rolled down her face. She turned her head to rub it away and hide her grief. A few rows behind, a tall and imposing man was gazing straight at her. Marion blushed and turned back to the front, to study the priest, who was still droning steadily on in unintelligible Latin.

One look into the heavenly, moist blue of this angel's eyes was all it took, Wallace was smitten. The young noble woman, two rows in front in St Kentigern's pews, was the most perfect woman he had ever seen.

After the service, as the good and the great of Lanark made their way from the church, followed by the tradespeople, William wasted no time in making her acquaintance. Helped by a couple of his friends, who came from the district and knew Marion and her family, the friendship grew quickly and unhindered. With no male family escort left alive to accompany her home, Marion dismissed her maid servant, who was shivering patiently in the church vestibule for her mistress. The delighted servant was given half a day of unexpected leave, to spend with her family. Meanwhile, Marion and two of Wallace's most trusted friends returned to the Castlegate, to have a meal together at Marion's home. As Marion shared her story of hardship and grief, having lost her family to the vicious war between Scotland and Edward's England, William knew that there would be no other woman for him now that he had met her.

Instantly their friendship blossomed into a love affair, Wallace worshipping the ground Lady Braidfute walked upon. Only eighteen years old, but grown wise so quickly through the troubled and turbulent times she was living in, Marion loved William back with all her heart. The Scottish cause for independence from Edward and his forces was still much in his mind, but the winter in Lanark with Marion gave Wallace and his men much-needed time to recuperate from their past skirmishes and grow their support and numbers in a canny, grassroots fashion. When Marion discovered she was pregnant, William married his sweetheart in the very church where he had first laid eyes upon her, at the top of Lanark High Street – St Kentigern's. The seeming normality of domestic, married life gave Wallace the cover he needed to plan his strategy for full-out war on the English and to build up the forces needed. At Marion's house in Castlegate,

Wallace had the perfect vantage point from which to watch the English garrison's operations just down the hill at Lanark Castle. Because the castle was old and wooden, the sheriff didn't stay there, instead occupying a much warmer and more comfortable stone house in the high street. Wallace observed Heselrig's movements carefully, waiting for the great reckoning day when he and his supporters could strike and take revenge.

Marion gave birth to a daughter and they named her Elizabeth. Despite the dreadful conditions of the occupation they were all living under, for a while they were blissfully happy together in Lanark with their baby girl. Then one fateful Sunday morning in May, as William strolled back from church along the Bloomgate, he passed a group of English soldiers who were heading back to their garrison. William ignored the jeering tone of one, who was mocking his sword, calling it a knife. Marion was at home with the baby and he wanted to be back with them as soon as possible, and although he was wearing his sword, he certainly didn't want a fight. William calmly ignored the soldiers and strode on, but then the soldiers taunted further.

'Isn't he the one that lives with that Scots whore at Castlegate?' snarled a toothless Englishman.

'Yeah,' replied another. 'When he goes out and leaves 'er at home wif the little bastard brat she had, the priest from the church next door goes in and gives 'er one! You know, absolves 'er of 'er carnal sins with his priesthood. Ee comes out lookin very happy.' The English fell about laughing, as more taunts about Marion, the priest and his daughter were jibbed at him. William could take no more and finally his temper snapped. His sword was drawn and moments later, the two slanderers were cut down, dead on the ground. The soldiers had rushed to defend themselves, but Wallace was fired up beyond abeyance, and limbs and bodies were dispatched with mighty blows from his sword. The sound of the fight brought more soldiers, but also some of Wallace's friends. In the space of fifteen minutes, fifty

English soldiers lay dead or wounded. William and his fighters had to flee, escaping to Marion's house. Soon the whole garrison were upon them. A barricade prevented the first onslaught, but Wallace was outnumbered. Out through the back and down through a neighbour's cellar was his only hope of escape.

Wallace and his friends did escape, evading capture by fleeing down the Brae and across to Cartland, where they hid in a cave, near the Mouse Water, then later to ancient underground dwellings that few know about even to this day.

Marion was not so lucky. When Heselrig discovered what had happened, he personally had Marion Braidfute dragged from her house into the Castlegate, where she was murdered before startled onlookers. Then the sheriff ordered the house to be set on fire with all the servants left inside to burn to death within. One quick-witted maid had already wrapped baby Elizabeth and escaped the same way William had. His daughter survived.

When William heard the news of his wife's slaughter, he vowed to take revenge on Heselrig. The English were, however, ready and waiting for the attack. But it didn't come. William took his time, gathering forces. Eventually Heselrig and his troops were convinced that the Scots fighter was just another coward who had given up – destroyed by grief perhaps? They didn't care, he was gone and the defences at Lanark sank into complacency.

William and his men sneaked into Lanark in the dead of night. William and a small group stormed the house where Heselrig lived on the high street, while the rest of Wallace's band overtook the castle guard and set the place on fire. In Heselrig's apartment, William split the sheriff's skull down to the collarbone with his enormous two-handed sword (he was a big man, over 6½ft tall). As Heselrig's son was awoken by the commotion and rushed to his father's apartment, he too was slaughtered. Young Auchinlek, one of William's followers, plunged his dagger into the almost lifeless body of Heselrig to make sure the villain was really dead! Wallace and his men killed over two hundred soldiers, merchants and commoners in the area around Lanark, sparing only women and priests. The town of Lanark and surrounds were left in a sorry state. The War of Independence in Scotland had only just begun.

All about the town of Lanark, you will find landmarks that bear the name of Wallace, the most famous of these being the cairn that sits proudly, like a giant nipple, on the top of Tinto Hill. A stone upon the hill has a large indentation, which local legend accredits to be the thumbprint of Wallace, this giant of a man, both literally in stature and a giant of Scottish history.

In Robert Chambers' *Popular Rhymes of Scotland* (1826) the rhyme of Tinto has been preserved for future generations to wonder about.

> On Tintock-tap there is a mist,
> And in that mist there is a kist [chest],
> And in the kist there is a caup [cup],
> And in the caup there is a drap [drop];
> Tak up the caup, drink aff the drap
> And set the caup on Tintock-tap.

It is assumed by Chambers that the hole in the stone is the cup in the kist, as it is often filled with rain water and it would truly take a supernatural giant to be able to pick it up and drink from it.

At Cartland Crags and along the deep gorge at the Falls of Clyde are two caves, both known as Wallace's Cave. Here according to legend, possibly fuelled more by past and present tourist industries than by historical accuracy, Wallace is supposed to have hidden from English troops.

WHUPPITY SCOORIE

The Wee Bell Ceremony takes place at St Nicholas's Church every year on 1 March, at 6 p.m. This custom is so old that no one actually knows when it began. When the bell starts to ring, a children's race around St Nicholas's commences. This event is called Whuppity Scoorie. The racers twirl a large paper ball attached to string around their heads. After completing three circuits around the church, there is a scramble for coins and sweets, provided by the local community council. In 1890 the *Hamilton Advertiser* mentioned, 'The lively variation of whuppit Scoorie,' and boys whirling their caps, attached to strings, around their heads and also using them as weapons. Around this time, the event became too boisterous, with clashes between the boys of New Lanark and the local policeman. Today, it is a much friendlier and happy event.

There are many suggestions as to why the people of Lanark decided to hold this highly unusual, annual celebration. The name Whuppity Scoorie was generally considered to be linked with the dust devils that blew about the streets and people's homes. Perhaps the custom comes from the very old, popular tradition of chasing away bad spirits by disturbing the air, and the clanging of the bell (metal drives away evil spirits) in the springtime, and thus ensuring a good harvest for the year ahead. Whippitie Stourie was another name for the brownie, who was usually a good spirit of the household, mill or farm.

The Tolbooth building in Lanark is close to the church and this is where the town cross once stood. Here prisoners were kept and wrongdoers attached to a high beam at the nearby Tron building as a punishment for their crimes. Around 1652, one poor woman, who had reported to the authorities that she had seen the eminent Major Thomas Weir of Waygateshaw House, near Carluke, committing an unspeakable act with a horse, was sentenced to be whipped around the town by the hangman for slandering such an eminent and holy man. The woman's indignation for telling the truth and not being believed must have been great, as Weir finally confessed to this bestiality years later at his trial for witchcraft in 1670.

Perhaps then, it was the whipping of all those unfortunate miscreants as punishment for their crimes during Lanark's dim and distant past that led to this strange ceremony, a mock whipping of malevolent forces. The similarly named Whoopity Stoorie is the title for one of the best-known Scots folk stories for children, from Dumfries and Galloway. Although Whoopity Stoorie doesn't turn out to be the witch in the tale's secret name, she is eventually defeated and chased off. Chasing the wicked away does seem to be the recurrent theme in this enigmatic Scottish expression.

THE GIRNIN DOG

Up on a gable end of number 15 Castlegate is a small, solid statue of a wee dog. Usually painted black and white – once with spots, like a Dalmatian – this creature has a curious story to tell.

In the early nineteenth century, during Lanark's flourishing textile days, John MacDonald, who was the deacon of the Dyers Trade Guild, applied to the town council for permission to build a new house for himself in a gap site next to Vere House in the Castlegate. Miss Mary Inglis, the owner of Vere House, strongly objected to MacDonald's plan. Her family had lived in Lanark since the 1600s, and at Vere House for at least two hundred years. It once belonged to the Veres of Stonebyres, a very old and influential family. All of the powerful families of the surrounding district who had castles and mansion houses in the countryside liked to have a townhouse in the Castlegate in Lanark.

Despite Miss Inglis's objection to the deacon's building plans, the council approved them. Mary Inglis was bitterly resentful that she was about to have a new house next to hers and a tradesman, John MacDonald, as a neighbour. She sat at her window each day drinking her morning tea, watching the bustle of daily life in the street below, and now she had to put up with construction workers, noise and dust.

MacDonald was on site to supervise the building of his new home, so Miss Inglis couldn't help but notice him striding about, giving orders. She also couldn't help but notice that he had a little pet dog with him whenever he visited the building site, and he appeared to be extremely fond of the animal.

MacDonald's new home was eventually finished and he moved in, with his trusty best friend, his little terrier. Miss Inglis still had her view of the Castlegate, but she also had MacDonald's property far closer to hers than she liked. She waited until she knew John MacDonald was away on a short business trip and then she took spiteful revenge against him.

The deacon returned home to find his faithful dog in the garden, dead. It didn't take him long to find out that his pet had been poisoned, and judging by the smirk on his neighbour's face when he caught sight of her the next morning, he knew that it was she who had killed his dog.

MacDonald did not give the vindictive woman the pleasure of witnessing his grief and anger any further. Instead, the canny deacon hired a stone-mason to make a statue of his terrier and had it posi-tioned on his gable, so that it was staring directly at Miss Inglis's window. It had a reproachful look on its face, its mouth open slightly in a grimace.

This is why it is called locally, the Girnin Dug. Mary Inglis would never be able to look from her window again without the animal's stony stare reminding her of her guilt.

Vere House was eventually demolished and a Lidl supermarket stands in its place today. No. 15 Castlegate with the statue of Deacon John MacDonald's pet dog is still there, watching and girnin over all who pass below.

11

WALLACE AND THE WRAITHS OF CLYDESDALE

A huge rock lies in the middle of the River Clyde, downriver from Stonebyre's Linn, between the villages of Kirkfieldbank and Hazelbank, in South Lanarkshire. This is the Carlin Stane, which was once famous with anglers for the quality of the trout that swam under its shady edges. Carlin stones are found all over Scotland – usually prehistoric standing stones or outstanding natural geological formations – the word 'Carlin' refers to an old woman, hag or witch, related to Calliach, the Hag of Winter, from the Irish and Scots tradition. An old rhyme from Lanarkshire relates that this Carlin Stane in the Clyde had its own mermaid:

The Mermaid sat on the Carlin stane,
A kaimen her gowden hair,
The May ne'er was in Clydesdale wide,
Was ever half sae fair.

(*The Scottish Journal of Topography*, 1847)

Long before William Wallace met and married Marion Braidfute,
when he was a young man, he spent much of his time at his
uncle's farm in South Lanarkshire. Gillbank, as it was known
then, eight hundred years ago, sat on the south bank of the
River Clyde, a couple of miles downstream from Lanark. Here,
William's main job was to look after his father's horses. It suited
his family to keep them here because of the abundant grazing
and the easy access to Lanark, where there was both a royal
racecourse and a weekly horse market. Life was not particularly
easy for the Scottish minor nobility and landowners at this time
because Scotland was occupied by King Edward I of England's
troops. While William lived in Lanarkshire, Lanark was occupied
by Heselrig, an English sheriff, and a platoon of his soldiers lived
at the old castle. Most families from the Scottish noble class tried
their best to keep out of his way, but young William enjoyed
taunting the occupiers at every opportunity.

Will was exceptionally tall and strong for his age and he
excelled in sports. Naturally, a garrison of the King's soldiers
had to stay prepared for war and fighting, so sports and games
were a regular part of their life. Will and other energetic youths
from Clydesdale were invited to take part in sporting events
and competitions held at the castle grounds by the English soldiers. Talented in all sports, Will enjoyed nothing more than
thrashing the Englishmen at wrestling, vaulting, racing, archery
and sword skills, but more than anything else, he loved to beat
them at putting the shot. Throwing a small cannonball over

exceptional distances was his forte and no one in Lanarkshire, or possibly even the entire country, could beat Will Wallace at the shot put. This annoyed the soldiers immensely. They enjoyed beating the Scots youth at sports, thus keeping them in their place; however, this particular young Scotsman was not only better at all of the games, but he had an arrogant and discourteous attitude towards them.

As their resentment at being beaten and ridiculed by Wallace grew, so did their desire to teach him a lesson to respect their authority. The soldiers set men to spy on William, watching his every move, so that they could devise a plan to put an end to his prowess on the sports fields.

The road that ran alongside the River Clyde and up the hill into Lanark was busy with carts, local folk, merchants, travellers and traders going about their daily business. On most days, William led his father's horses across this road, down to the ford near Dublin Bridge and over to the south-facing slope of the Nemphlar Brae. The grass grew so much lusher on the sunny side of the valley than on the shadier folds of the Kirkfield bank where Wallace lived. Tending a herd of grazing horses could have been very tedious to a lad of Will's age, but he had a quick and curious mind and always made the best of his tasks. While the herd moved with the sun across the hillside, Will liked to scramble up and down the cliffs and banks of the Clyde, occasionally checking back in on the horses to make sure they were safe. His favourite spot was just below the waterfalls of Stone Byres. When there was plenty of rainfall the Linn would thunder with the surge of water pouring over the succession of rocky drops. William loved to climb out on to a prominent precipice of land that hung over the river, downstream of the falls. Here he would lie on his stomach with his head and neck craned out to catch the shower of water spraying up from the tumulus below. Even on days of low water levels and gentler currents, William still enjoyed sitting on the overhang, looking

far down the river and road in both directions – watching who
came and went along the valley. Unknown to William, two
English spies had concealed themselves at the Linn Mill on
the opposite bank of the river and had observed all of his daily
chores. They reported his habit of sitting on the overhang back
to their garrison commander and a wicked plan was hatched
that would end William's sporting days once and for all. The
day finally arrived when William came face to face with his fate.

He woke early, as the sun rose in the east and flooded the
land with golden light. After a hearty breakfast of porridge,
Will gladly gathered the horses, tethered them loosely together
and set off down the hill towards the river. He met no one as
he crossed over the road and rode through the shallow water to
the track along the other side of the Clyde. It was too early for
people to be going about their business, Will and his horses were
alone in the valley except for a family of ducks who quacked
cheekily as the horses splashed past their nest. He enjoyed
a leisurely stroll up and down the rocky path, passing the
Stone Byres' Linns, until he reached the best grazing ground.
Dismounting from his own horse, he set the herd to graze contentedly across the sunlit brae. Then, Will turned and headed
for his favourite lookout post, high above the river. Carefully, he
picked his way through brambles and between hazel trees until
he was near the jagged outcrop of rocks that jutted out over the
river gorge. But just as William put his foot on to the ground
of the overhang, he was startled by movement from behind a
gorse bush in front of him. An old woman appeared, stepping
away from the thicket and turning to look at William. As she
stood between him and the cliff edge, she held up her hand,
motioning for William to stop. She was dressed like any elderly
grandmother of the day, with a long dark skirt, woollen jacket,
and matching bonnet, tied neatly under her chin. She calmly
held William's gaze with her wrinkled, wise eyes, and pointed
her finger slowly at the ground. She pointed decisively at each

of the rocks and the earth that delineated where the overhang met with solid ground. She shook her head in an authoritative and solemn manner, then disappeared. William stood, wide-eyed, staring at the space where the old woman had vanished. Immediately, he realised that she must be from the spirit world and that she was warning him to keep back from the river. He took the supernatural message seriously and made his way back to the Brae to guard the horses.

The next day, William drove the horses to the Braes, keen to go back to the place he had seen the spectre. After an evening of sharing his ghostly sighting with his family, he was determined to be less timid and speak with the woman if she appeared again.

Once the horses were settled, he raced to the cliff edge, and sure enough as he approached the large overhang, the woman appeared. Her manner seemed more urgent than before as she raised her hands to stop William from coming nearer. Before he could speak, she walked out of sight behind the gorse bush, then reappeared with someone else beside her. William gasped, as he recognised the man with her – it was himself! The spectral William moved to the place where the precipice joined the solid land, raised a large rock above his head and threw it down upon the ground. Both the woman and other William Wallace pointed at this patch of land, turned urgently to stare directly at the real William, then together they vanished into thin air. Young William stood for a moment, transfixed by the strange vision, then he jumped to action, knowing exactly what he must do. He made his way to the spot where the other William had stood, and staying on the firm edge of the precipice, Will found a large rock, which he threw with all his strength, down on to the exact place the apparition had thrown his stone. Immediately, the ground began to shudder and tremble. William stepped back-wards, his boot catching a large turf of recently cut earth. As the sod dislodged, William could see a line of cut turf that had been carefully placed back over the undermined overhang. This was the same line in the ground that the woman had inspected the day before. Will picked up another boulder and with an almighty throw, dashed it down on to the weakened structure. This time, the whole cliff edge creaked and groaned and gave way in a tremendous avalanche of rocks, earth and vegetation, plummeting down into the deep river gorge below.

That evening, young William Wallace had an extraordinary tale to tell his family. The ground had clearly been dug away by the devious English soldiers, who had planned for Wallace to fall to his death in the water below. But William had been saved by the spirit of an old woman and his own wraith, his guardian genii. This incident helped to fuel William's desire to free Scotland from the occupying enemy even further. The edge of the fallen cliff now sat firmly in the middle of the River Clyde. Its supernatural association with the wraiths of Clydesdale and many stories that grew around the rock since William Wallace lived in the valley over eight hundred years ago – like that of the golden-haired mermaid – helped earn it the title of the Carlin Stane. It is still there today, just below the Stonebyres Hydro-Electric Power Station.

NB: Gillbank's name changed, at some point, over the many centuries since this story was told, and is now called Kilbank.

12

KATIE NEEVIE'S HOARD

According to Robert Chamber's Popular Rhymes of Scotland, *there is a very old rhyme from South Lanarkshire, which goes:*

Between Dillerhill and Crossfoord
There lies Katie Neevie's hoord

This little rhyme refers to a location in South Lanarkshire, which lies close to Blackhill View Point, near Lesmahagow, overlooking the Clyde Valley. In fact, it is right opposite my house!

This is a story of ancient hill forts, a standing stone, buried treasure and a clever, Lanarkshire lass.

Katie Neevie was born and brought up in the parish of Lesmahagow. Nobody would have thought there was anything different about her, just an ordinary country girl who worked on her parent's smallholding. She took the cows to pasture in the morning, milked them by evening, and helped her mother to make cheese in the dairy. But one day something so special happened to Katie that it changed her life forever, and she would never be considered an 'ordinary' country lass again.

Katie followed the parish customs like all the other young, unmarried men and woman of her time. At Beltane, the first day of May, Katie went with her friends to the hill where the ceremonial May Day bonfire was held. This was an ancient calendar celebration, which belonged to old ways that neither Katie nor her pals knew much about. The fact that the ritual bonfire and customary gathering was part of the old pagan religious tradition was of no interest to Katie's generation, they went purely to enjoy the dancing, singing and each other's high-spirited company. The Beltane fire for the people of Lesmahagow and surrounding farm touns was held on Black Hill, which was the site of an ancient hill fort. Early settlers had built their fortress home here as far back as the Bronze Age, and continued to live there right through the Iron Age, too. Situated on the west bank of the Clyde Valley, it formed part of a ridge of small hills that led to the largest, Tinto Hill, in the south.

On Beltane evening, Katie and her family walked the boundaries of their rig of land, scattering spring water and salt at the edges and reciting a blessing for protection and good harvest. Next, the women blessed the cows in the byre with spring water and tied a knot of plaited horse hair, ribbon and dried rowan berries neatly into each cow's tail. Katie then washed her face and braided her hair in readiness for the night out, while her brother and father teased her about 'looking pretty enough to charm the crows from the trees!' Her mother and gran caught her in the doorway, and made a fuss as they inspected her. Her mother warned her to avoid drunkards and to be home before it was time to milk the cows, while Gran wrapped a woollen shawl around Katie's shoulders and pinned her special Celtic broach to it. Gran kissed Katie goodnight and pushed a posy of aromatic herbs into her apron pocket for good luck.

She stood on the doorstep, watching and quietly chanting an old blessing, as her granddaughter ran off down the path towards the village. Katie met up with her friends at the market cross and, laughing and chattering, they all set off across the burn and over the fields towards Dillerburn. There, they turned off the roadway and began the steep climb up the slope of Black Hill, towards the summit. Here, among the old earthworks and scattered stones of the ancient hill fort, was a newly constructed pile of dried tree branches, old gorse boles, and bits of wooden barns and sheds that the local farmhands had donated towards the bonfire. Katie's grandmother often told her the story of how she had met and fallen in love with her husband, Morton – Katie's grandfather – many, many years before, at the May Day fire. Gran liked to talk about the thrill of seeing the bonfire being lit on Tinto Hill, to the south, which burned the largest and brightest and could be seen for many miles, connecting all of these ancestral fires across Scotland. Perhaps it was because of her gran's love of the stories about the old tribes who had lived and were now buried under the hill forts, or maybe it was the excitement of the music, dancing, cider drinking and flirting, but Katie took a giddy turn not long after the fire was lit. Her friends caught her as she collapsed and lay her on a blanket on the ground a little way from the fire. Katie's head span and she had to close her eyes and take long, slow breaths. While she relaxed and let the feeling of dizziness pass, Katie had a vision of a king lying immediately beneath her, under the hill. It felt as if she was entering a dream, but Katie could still hear the merriment of the party and her friend's concerned comments about her faint. She felt her body slipping down through the earth and stones, into a chamber below, where she could see the recumbent king, in full armour, lying peacefully in a stone coffin. On his head was a golden crown, covered in sparkling gems. Katie opened her eyes to see the blacksmith's son's face looming over her. She pulled herself back from the strange, trance-like vision of being underground, sat up and slapped the cheeky lad, who was trying his luck to kiss her. Katie recovered her wits and composure and soon felt steady enough to join the party again. The evening continued joyously into the small hours of the morning, when the tired revellers either fell asleep where they had fallen or returned home to their own beds.

Katie felt oddly disturbed by her strange experience and was curious to find out if her vision might hold some truth; so the next day, after her chores, she collected two spades and went with her younger brother back to the top of the hill. No one was there now, the last remaining Beltane merrymakers had taken their hangovers down to the village inn, to treat their thumping heads with a hair of the dog cure. Katie led her brother to the place where she had felt herself slipping into the underground burial site. Here, next to a great circle of charred ground and the remains of the ceremonial fire, she felt a tingle run up her spine. Katie pushed her shovel into the earth, the tingle whizzed through her arm and into her ears, making her tremble all over.

'Here, Georgie boy! This is the place I saw it, and I can feel something strange running through me. Get to work with that spade!' Together, brother and sister dug into the old hill fort for all they were worth. After digging for almost an hour, when Katie thought she couldn't manage to lift her shovel one more time, her brother pulled out a piece of broken pot from the earth. They inspected the clay fragment with excitement. Then they dropped to their knees and, using their hands, scraped the soil away in scoops and furrows. As they moved the dark crumbly dirt from the hole, they began to find many pieces of broken pottery. This convinced them both that it was worth the effort to keep excavating the ground. Eventually, the earth collapsed on one side of the trench they had made and Katie's brother slid down into a stone kist below. The astonished siblings found a complete skeleton, many other bones and pottery inside the kist. They sifted through the shards, until Katie nicked her finger on something sharp. Wiping dirt and blood from the cut, she grinned at her brother and said, 'I've found it Georgie! Help me here, it's a box or something!'

As she scraped and tugged at the ancient object, joined quickly by George's strong hands, a small metal casket emerged from the earth. They examined it, brushing off the soil from its lid. As Katie picked off more impacted clay dirt, beautiful ornate patterns appeared on the surface of the chest – a skinny dog, someone riding on a horse, birds and foliage – long ago sculpted into the metalwork. A clasp broke and fell away from the box. Katie pressed and pulled until she managed to prise open the lid. Inside gleamed golden necklaces, rings and bracelets, untarnished, as yellow and bright as the day they were made. With racing hearts, the pair felt as though they had discovered the wealth of the world. They continued to dig around the stone burial chamber and after much work they unearthed a fortune in Celtic burial treasure.

When they had gathered everything they could find and laid it on the grass, the brother and sister sat down to rest their aching bodies and make a sensible plan. Katie was no fool, she knew that there was very little a lass like her could do with such a fortune, and even less that her fourteen-year-old brother could do. He would most likely be accused of stealing it!

'We must hide this treasure again George, and I will think of a way to sell it without us getting into trouble. Perhaps Gran will be able to help us, she is the wisest person I know. But we are going to have to keep this secret from everyone else. If anyone finds out we have so much gold, why, I think they would murder us for it.'

George agreed with his sister and they decided that he should stay on the hill and fill in the holes, while Katie ran to fetch something in which to hide their secret hoard. Before she left the burial site, Katie went back to the skeleton in the stone coffin and gingerly removed the skull from its resting place. Gran had taught her that water sipped from a cup made of a human skull was meant to cure madness and, therefore, it was a very useful healing tool to have. She carefully wrapped the ancient head in her scarf and, saying a quiet prayer of thanks, put it inside her apron. Then she sprinted back down the hill to her home. She wasted no time stashing the skull under her bed, collecting a sheepskin and an old sack from the byre and her mother's leaking kettle, which had sat out in the yard collecting rain water. She returned to George, who had filled in the earthworks and scattered the bonfire ashes over the area to cover up any signs of digging. They filled the sheepskin with the larger golden ornaments, the sack with the metal casket and the kettle with amulets and coins. Then they thought about where to hide their fortune. They looked down at the hamlet of houses in Lesmahagow and could think of no safe hiding places there, far too many folk lived in the village! Turning east towards Stonebyres Wood and the great River Clyde, they scanned the farms and cottages scattered about the surrounding countryside. Remembering all of the places they had played in and explored as children, they carefully selected the best secret nooks and crannies in which to conceal their booty.

Clever Katie, perhaps guided by her wise grandmother and definitely supported by her loyal brother, kept her cool and her fortune. George built a mill and the family prospered and thrived. Katie's fame spread far and wide during her lifetime. Of course it did, she was a wealthy woman. She never forgot the old ways and went every year to the Beltane and New Year bonfires. Katie remembered why and how her luck had come to her, and was for ever grateful to the people and traditions of the past.

Somehow, over many centuries, Katie's tale became linked with witchcraft and devil worship; the old pagan beliefs being merged with the occult and Satanism. Katie NicNevin was the name that became synonymous with Scotland's most notorious head witch. Stories were told of a powerful female who gathered with youths at the ceremonial tides of the year and danced before blazing fires on hillsides and beaches. Was Katie NicNevin a head witch, or was she perhaps a strong, independent woman, like Katie Neevie from Lesmahagow?

Over time, local Lanarkshire legends hinted at her treasure being hidden under the great standing stone at the bottom of

Black Hill, on the road to Dillerburn – maybe, during their lifetime, Katie and George teased gullible folk into thinking they had hidden their treasure here, knowing that no one would be able to move the great stone obelisk.

However, the legend of Katie's buried treasure grew over time, and many treasure hunters attempted to find it in the quiet Lanarkshire hamlet near Dillerhill. Over many centuries, a story unfolded of a curse on the standing stone. Rumour spread that there was a portal to hell under the stone. Those who attempted to dig up the hoard reported that the Devil himself sprang up from beneath the immense rock and engulfed them in flames.

At some point in the eighteenth century, a farmer, James Prentice of Clerkston Farm, managed to entice a couple of Irish farm workers who had been helping with the harvest to brave the curse and look for the buried treasure. Impressed by the old stories of how rich Katie and her family were, and that some of their wealth was still hidden under the giant stone, the labourers each said a prayer to God for protection, and set about breaking and splintering the great rock. In case the fiery demon sprang up, the men made a rota, one digging, while the other kept watch with a loaded pistol. After a full day of smashing rock and hard graft, the Devil did not make an appearance and no buried treasure was found.

Katie had clearly hidden her treasure in a much safer place! Mr Prentice, however, did get the standing stone reduced to smaller-sized rocks, but perhaps the place is cursed and the pile of rocks is guarded by the Devil, because it is still there today, clearly visible at the edge of a field, waiting for someone brave enough, or daft enough, to try moving it.

13

THE LOCKHARTS' LUCKY PENNY

The Lee Valley sits below Lanark on the north of the River Clyde. Here is Lee Castle where the Lockhart family (formerly Lockhard) lived for many years. Their name changed after Sir Simon Lockhard travelled with Sir James Douglas and other Scottish knights on a pilgrimage to the Holy Lands with Robert the Bruce's heart. This is the story.

Pilgrimage to the Holy Land was high on the wish list of every Scottish knight and nobleman, especially if, like King Robert Bruce, there were sins to be forgiven. Robert didn't have time to make the pilgrimage while he was still alive, as most of his time was taken up with fighting off Edward I and England's invading armies. He did, however, want more than anything to make his peace with God for having killed John Comyn, especially as it had been inside a chapel! As Robert lay dying, his most trusted friend Sir James Douglas by his side, he asked James to cut out his heart after he was dead and to take it to the Holy City for burial, so that his sins would be atoned for before God. The ever faithful James did as the great King had wished and after the Bruce had passed away, his heart was cut out, wrapped up carefully and enclosed in a silver casket. A group of knights volunteered for the

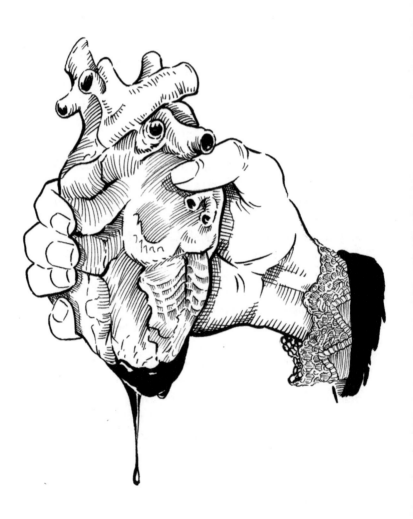

great journey to Palestine and they began this most important of pilgrimages, with their very special casket.

Among the pilgrims was Sir Simon Lockhard of Lee, another of the King's most fervent supporters. His special task was to carry the silver key that opened the casket holding the Bruce's heart. In the year 1330, the men set out with solemn thoughts on a long and arduous journey.

As they made their way along the well-travelled pilgrims' routes towards the east, they became involved in a war between the Spanish and the Moors. The King of Spain asked for their help to drive the Moorish invaders from Spain. The Scots fighters gave their support to the Spaniards willingly, but things took a turn for the worse when they ran into an ambush devised by the Moors. Seeing his comrade William St Clair of Roslin being cut down from his horse, James Douglas rushed to help him, but was also overpowered and killed. When this battle at Teevor was over, many lay dead, including several of the Scottish lords. Those who remained retrieved the silver casket, with its precious cargo, along with the bodies of their slain men. Sir Simon and the rest of the Scots decided that, with their party so depleted, they would not risk journeying any further, but instead would return home to Scotland.

The casket with the Bruce's heart was buried at Melrose Abbey. As the casket's key-keeper, Sir Simon changed his family name from Lockhard to Lockhart. This he did in honour of his noble King and in undying allegiance to an independent Scotland, and as a faithful friend to Robert the Bruce.

The Bruce's heart and a new name were not the only things that Simon Lockhart brought back from his travels. At the Battle of Teevor, among the captured was a Saracen prince. Lockhart had set a high ransom for the release of this wealthy emir. While the emir's mother had handed over the large sum demanded in silver and gold coins, a small red stone had fallen from her money bags. Sir Simon had noticed how quick the woman was to pick it up and hide it away. Simon demanded to see the stone, but the prince's mother was very reluctant to show it to him. He insisted that her son would not be released until he had satisfied his curiosity and had seen what this amulet was. After much argument, she finally handed over a small, triangular semi-precious stone. It wasn't particularly remarkable to look at and it certainly wasn't a ruby or any other precious gem. The woman explained that it was a healing stone, which when dipped and swirled in water would give healing powers to the water that could then cure cattle, horses and even people of many diseases. Sir Simon liked the idea of this very much and insisted that it become part of the payment for her son's freedom. She had no other choice than to give it up to the Scottish lord.

Back at Lee Castle, the little red stone was set into an Edward I silver shilling. It began its work as a cure for livestock under much speculation from the nobleman and his family, but soon good results were reported from the head livestock keeper. This special talisman, or Lee Penny as it came to be called, went on to have a great reputation for incredible healing and restorative powers.

The dreaded plague ravaged Newcastle, and the elders of the city sent for the penny, paying a bond of £1,000 for its safe return. The City Corporation then offered the Lockhart of the time a further £6,000 to be able to keep the penny, but he declined. Lady Baird of Saughtonhall, near Edinburgh, was given loan of the stone so that she could drink the water in which it had been dipped and bathe in baths to cure her from hydrophobia, contracted from the bite of a rabid dog. She was indeed cured. Eventually, the stone was considered so valuable that rather than let it out of the family's castle and possession, they would only allow cure seekers to come to them to dip the stone in the water, which they then could carry home. The visitors included a farmer who came from Northumberland on his horse with four small barrels, which were filled with the water anointed with the Lee Penny, and a Yorkshire farmer who needed to cure his cattle, which had been bitten by a mad dog.

The curing penny was used for many centuries. Its silver coin was replaced with a newer coin in the late fifteenth century, a groat from the London Mint, dating from the reign of Edward IV. After the Reformation, belief in such cures was considered Catholic and devilish, but even the Church made an exception for the Lee Penny as long as no charms or words were spoken in relation to its use.

The last time a story of the penny's healing powers was told was when, in the 1920s, Lord Lockhart was out with a shooting party. Over lunch, there was no bottle opener to open the beer, so one gentleman took out his penknife and prised a bottle open. The knife slipped and cut him deeply. The wound was wrapped, but by night-time it was still bleeding profusely. Not wanting to incur the cost of hiring the local doctor, Lord Lockhart suggested the penny. It was placed in a bowl of water and the stone was swirled around in it. Next bandages were dipped in the water and wrapped tightly over the wound. It is said that by the very next morning, the cut had miraculously knitted together and was dry.

It is no wonder that with such magical abilities and enduring history, Sir Walter Scott wrote a novel called *The Talisman* about this very special jewel.

14

THE BLACK
CLYDESDALE HORSE

The Clydesdale Horse is one of Scotland's most impressive horse breeds. Scottish breeders produced these tall, strong horses to meet the demands of the construction industry in the growing cities and booming agricultural developments of the eighteenth and nineteenth centuries. They were bred originally in the early eighteenth century from the sixth Duke of Hamilton's six, black Flemish stallions with ordinary farm mares of Lanarkshire by a breeder named John Paterson, of Lochlyoch in Carmichael. The breed was developed in the Clydesdale area, which it is named after, with support from local breeders, and others in Glasgow, Galloway and Aberdeenshire. Standing at seventeen hands high, with a thick mane, feathered feet and shaggy coat that suited the Scottish climate, these docile horses had the largest horseshoe fitting of any horse in the world. They were considered to be the most efficient ploughing and pulling animal on the planet. Between 1885 and the start of the Second World War, twenty thousand Clydesdales were exported all over the world. A legendary sale for one horse took place in 1911 at Lanark Market. Five thousand people came to the sale, where two bidders began a bidding war for a twelve-year-old Clydesdale stallion called Baron of Buchlyvie. He sold for the

*world record price of £9,500. Baron's skeleton is now displayed at
Kelvingrove Museum in Glasgow.*

*They are still bred in Lanarkshire. I counted four foals at Dillars
Clydesdale stud farm just the other day.*

*I first heard this story of the Black Clydesdale at a storytelling
club in Lanark in 2008. Charlotte Howat from Howgate Farm,
near Carluke, told us this true story about one of her father's horses
– he was a farmer and had a passion for breeding Clydesdales.
Later, Charlotte let me record her telling the tale and recounting
her experiences of growing up in a farming community.*

This is Charlotte's story.

When Charlotte was just a wee girl, barely old enough to
have started school, her favourite chore was helping to get her
father's horses ready for the big agricultural shows. Her mother
would heat up kettles of water on the range in the kitchen,
then mix these with cold water in metal buckets in the yard.
Charlotte and her sister would carry the buckets to the stables,
where her father and Robert the dairy man would assign each
girl a horse. All of the farm horses were Clydesdales, great tall
beasts of around seventeen hands high. They were so huge that
Charlotte could almost stand up underneath their rounded,
hairy bellies. The children had to wash their manes, forelocks,
fetlocks and tails by taking a sponge to large blocks of soap
until they had a mountain of foaming lather and applying it to
the thick coarse hair of their allotted horse. Some horses would
shake their heads vigorously, spraying warm, wet bubbles over
everything, including the humans who were standing near
them. Others stamped their hooves and whinnied loudly to
their companions in neighbouring stalls. Most of the horses
enjoyed the pampering. Charlotte's dad always gave the
calmest and gentlest animals to her and her sister, while the
men washed the lively ones. Gallons of water were splashed
about the stalls, among a lot of banter and laughter. The tall,

muscular horses sensed the fun and excitement, and seemed to enjoy the fuss and attention as much as Charlotte loved shampooing and brushing them.

When heads, legs and tails were scrubbed thoroughly, what was left of the soapy water was brushed through the creatures' coats. Once all of the warm water had gone, Robert led each horse out into the yard. As he held them firmly by their head collars, father turned on the cold water hosepipe and the soapy beast was given a good shower. Rivers of suds and rainbow-tinged foam poured down on to the cobblestones from their dripping coats. During this part of the animals' ablutions, Charlotte and her sister ducked down, hiding behind a stable door. But wherever they sheltered, either her father or Robert would find the girls and squirt the hose in their direction, drenching them in freezing water. They always ended up just as wet as the animals. During their cold shower and final rinse, the horses became vocal and boisterous. Robert stood calmly by their heads whispering soothing words into their ears. Next the children took dry rags and sackcloth and climbed up on to old wooden crates, so that they could reach the top of the horse's shoulders and hindquarters and rub away the excess water. The huge animals shivered and shook themselves to rid their coats of dampness, Charlotte and her sister getting yet another soaking in the process. As more dry hessian was rubbed along muscular necks, shoulders and large curvy rumps, the creatures snorted with pleasure. The massage left their hairy coats smooth, clean and gleaming. Finally, the beautiful beasts were tied to the stock fence, where they could bask, their hair drying off in the sunny yard. Charlotte combed through the manes, making sure all were tangle free and perfectly smooth. By the time the whole operation was over, each animal was spotless and the colours in their coats, manes and tails was glossy and vibrant in the sunshine. The men finished by painting the hooves with special linseed oil. The feathers around their feet had become bouffant and fluffy. Each horse stood proud, shiny in radiant equine perfection.

As the tack was cleaned, the excitement of a show day just kept growing. Then, it was the people's turn to wash and get dressed in their Sunday best. When the horses were loaded into the lorry, mother and baby sister would appear from the farmhouse, mum in her good jacket and hat, with a big hamper of sandwiches and treats. There were always boiled sweeties for the journey to the showground, shared out among the family and workers. For Charlotte, these were the most enjoyable days of the summer and farming year. However, one year, when Charlotte was ten years old, a new Clydesdale horse came to the farm who was quite different to any other her father had bought before.

To begin with, this mare was jet black, which was highly unusual for the breed. She was named Queenie. At first, her father could do nothing with Queenie. Even going into the stall to harness the horse was impossible; her eyes would roll, she would fling back her head and bare her teeth at the farmer. No matter how gently or meekly he approached her, the horse took fright and lashed out at him with teeth and hooves. The farm workers teased Charlotte's dad, telling him that he'd obviously lost his touch with horses and it was time for him to retire and let them sort the animal out. But when they tried to gain the black horse's trust, they had even less luck than he'd had. Queenie reared up, biting and kicking at anyone who entered her stall, no matter how many carrots and apples they tried to placate her with. Over time, Queenie began to settle down and to trust Charlotte's dad. He loved his horses and knew how to bring them on with kindness and patience. After a few weeks she was working well for him, but Charlotte's mum didn't trust Queenie and felt too anxious about having her three little girls running around the farm with this crazy horse about. Charlotte and her sisters were told never to go near Queenie, but they couldn't resist sneaking into the barn and spying on the beautiful creature through the slits in the wall. When Queenie saw the children, she would stamp her hooves and bare her teeth at them. One day, her father took Charlotte and her sister into the stable and showed them Big Jock's teeth. Jock was a huge, placid bay Clydesdale, who you could do anything with. Her father said, 'See how big Jock's teeth are – now Queenie's are twice as big, and she bites!'

One day, when Charlotte's mother was crossing the farmyard, she happened to look over at Queenie in the stable. The horse lowered her head for a moment, acknowledging her presence, but then she flung her head around, as if she'd seen something in the yard invisible to the human eye. She screamed loudly, rising on to her back legs and kicking against the stable door. As metal shoes struck the cobbles, sparks flew out from under the door. Charlotte's mother shivered and pulled her cardigan tightly around her as the poor animal shrieked and battered her stall with powerful kicks. That evening, Charlotte overheard her mother telling her father that the mare would never settle there, she didn't think it was safe for the children, and he was to get shot of the horse.

It came as no surprise to the family when father announced the following day that he was taking the animal to the next Clydesdale sale at Lanark Market. When the sale day arrived, Father and the men had to give Queenie her shampoo and set. Charlotte and her sisters watched from the safety of the farmhouse doorstep. As the men tried to wash her feet she squealed and kicked. Pails went flying out of the stable, and Charlotte heard the men calling Queenie everything but a horse! Her mother hurried the girls inside the house, refusing to let them see or hear any more. Charlotte slipped quietly to her bedroom to watch the final fun out of the window, as Robert and her father tried to lead the mare into the truck. Queenie refused to go in until they put a sack over her head and subdued her. With two men on either side, they pulled and cajoled her up the ramp into the truck. The doors were shut and away they went. The excitement was over. Mother reassured the children, 'It's this place girls! That horse has never been at ease in this farm, she would never have settled here. It's right to sell her.'

When Charlotte's father and Robert got back from Lanark Market they described how nervous they had both felt as they unloaded Queenie into the pen at the market. Potential buyers came round to inspect the horses, running their hands over the animals' backs, down their legs, picking up and checking the hooves and looking at the horses' teeth. Robert said he reckoned he'd 'lost a stone in weight, he was that anxious!' But to everyone's surprise, Queenie had stood, as good as gold, without moving a muscle, while folk looked her over. Father told the family that the mare had sold quickly and for a very good price. He felt terrible though and guilty about selling such a devil horse to another honest farmer like himself. He reckoned that she would be back when the buyer discovered how wild she was.

But she never did come back to Charlotte's farm. From then on, at market on Mondays, Charlotte's father avoided all contact with the chap to whom he had sold the horse. One day, though, he felt a tap on his shoulder, he turned round and there he was, the farmer who'd bought Queenie!

'Why on earth did you sell a horse like that?' the man asked him.

Trying to think on his feet, Charlotte's father grinned sheepishly and said, 'Well, I could'ny keep them all!' The man looked him straight in the eye and said, 'She's the best horse I have ever had. The best-natured, hardest-working and best-looking mare. My son works with her, she's fantastic!' He shook Charlotte's father's hand, and thanked him again for selling him such a wonderful horse. When her father got home that day and told the family what had happened, everyone was astonished to hear the surprisingly good news about Queenie. Charlotte's mother repeated her words of wisdom.

'That horse would never have been content here, it was something about this place. Horses can see a world that's far beyond our ken, and whatever that animal was seeing here upset her and brought out her wildness. Queenie belonged somewhere else and now she's happy, and that was all that was wrong with that horse, she didn't like this place!'

THE MIDDLE WARD

15

THE BLUE FLAME OF STRATHAVEN

This story belongs to a collection of tales described in Chambers' Popular Rhymes of Scotland *as Money Digging Rhymes (p.236). It is similar to Katie Neevie's Hoard, except this chap from Strathaven is not so lucky as Katie.*

The lands of Carnduff lie to the north-west of the town. Strathaven is a very attractive, historic market town, complete with a ruined castle and village green. It's close to the A71 on the main route between Kilmarnock and Edinburgh and well worth a visit to enjoy the annual Air Balloon Festival, great pubs and eateries in well-preserved, colourful buildings.

Once, there was a poor farmhand from Strathaven, who woke one night from a vivid dream. He had heard a voice, as clear as a bell, which said:

Dig the ground at Carnduff
There you'll find gold enough.

And in his dream he saw a fast-flowing burn, a thorn tree, and a pickaxe sticking out from a big tuft of grass.

He opened his eyes and sat up in his bed. The vision had seemed so real and the voice had sounded as though it was in the room right next to him. He looked about the tiny room, but saw nothing unusual, so he settled back to sleep and thought no more of it. That is, until the next night when once again, he was woken by an even louder voice, saying:

Dig the ground at Carnduff
You're sure to find gold enough.

And once again, in the dream he could see clearly the small hawthorn tree and the burn, with a fork sticking up from coarse grass in front of a thicket. He woke up, rubbed his eyes and looked around the room to see if someone was playing tricks on him, hiding in the shadows. But there was no one there, just his wife snoring gently next to him. He let out an exasperated sigh, pulled the covers over his head, shut his eyes tightly and went back to sleep.

The dream came back again on the third night. The voice was louder than ever,:

DIG THE GROUND AT CARNDUFF
YOU'RE SURE TO FIND GOLD ENOUGH.

He woke his wife and asked her if she had heard anything. She grumbled that she hadn't, rolled over and went back to sleep. He lay awake thinking, if a dream should come to haunt him three nights in a row then maybe he should pay heed to its message. The picture of the burn, the tree and fork had been clear as crystal in his mind, perhaps it was time to follow his dream.

The next day he set off along the back road to the place where the farms of Carnduff are spread out across the land. He carried a spade and pickaxe with him. After walking some distance he eventually reached the Black Burn. Here he turned and followed the water up towards its source. The grass became rough moorland. Here, grazing sheep lifted their heads to stare at him, before dashing away, bleating in their panic. Eventually he spotted a thorn tree growing on the banks of the burn, which looked very similar to the one in his dream. When he noticed a big tussock of coarse, brown grass growing in front of the hawthorn tree, he chuckled out loud.

'I reckon this is the very spot frae ma dream! An I'll just get oan wi it, and do as the voice telt me!'

With that, he swung his pickaxe with all his strength and began digging into the tough vegetation on the upland moor. He dug the uncultivated ground for almost an hour, all the time sweating profusely and panting with the exertion. He paused occasionally, cupping his hands into the burn to take a draught of the cool, refreshing water.

Just when he thought he hadn't the strength to swing his pick, or dig with his shovel any more, a stone fell from the pile of loose earth, tumbled down into the huge hole he had made and hit something solid at the bottom with a resounding clunk.

He threw his shovel aside, bent down on his hands and knees, and groped about with both hands in the bottom of the pit. A · solid circle of baked clay was revealed in the dark crumbly soil. Frantically, he swept the sliding earth away from the object to reveal a big earthenware lid. Pushing his fingers down below the rim of the clay lid, he felt smooth, rounded sides of what must be a monster-sized urn below his hands. He had found it, the buried gold. It must be here inside this pot!

He yelled for joy and began scraping the soil away from around the great urn. Suddenly, from further up the hill there was an ear-splitting crack and a high-pitched wail echoed all around. The labourer covered his ears with his muddy hands, trying to block out the unearthly screaming, which was loud enough to burst his eardrums. To his astonishment, an explosion of bright blue flame erupted from the rocky crag above him. It sounded like a hundred snakes hissing violently, as blue flames spat ferociously from between the boulders. An otherworldly voice cried out from within the dancing azure fire:

Nothing but harm will come to you,
If that lid you unscrew.
The gold you seek, lies o'er the lee,
South O' Carnduff hill you'll see,
A lone gnarled oak, growing sparse,
Dig in front the tuft of grass,
And there gold you will find,
So your pockets will aye be lined.

The flame continued to spark and hiss all about the crag above. Terrified that it might shoot its blue flames down and consume him, he clambered out of the hole, grabbed up his tools and stumbled away towards South Carnduff. Checking over his shoulder to make sure nothing supernatural was following him, he trekked across hill, moor and farmland, until he came to a stunted oak tree. Sure enough, the trunk had been pollarded into three old stems, and in front of the tree grew a big tuft of grass.

Again, he laboured and sweated, digging up the untilled, rock-hard ground among the roots of the oak. As the sun began setting, he realised that the daylight was fading fast and his energy was spent. There wasn't an ounce of strength left in him to dig any more. He threw his tools down, cursing angrily. The thought struck him that maybe the speaking flame had tricked him and the gold really was in the clay urn, back at the burn. Once more, he picked up his shovel and axe and traipsed over the hill and moor back to the first treasure site. He found the hawthorn tree near the burn, but where was the freshly dug ground? He was sure it was here, at this gnarled, spiny thorn bush, but there was definitely no hole nor sign of digging. The wretched man stormed up and down searching frantically beside the Black Burn. He thought he was going mad – had his dream brought him to this lonely hillside, or was he dreaming now? Not only had the great pit vanished, but the ground lay seemingly undisturbed, the turf and grass growing exactly as he had found it earlier that morning. As the light dwindled into darkness, he gave up his search for the pot of gold, and dragged his weary limbs back home to his worried wife.

It didn't take long for the farmhand's strange story to spread throughout the neighbourhood. A few adventurous young-sters and folk desperate for money made the expedition over the moorland to a wild thorny bush, next to the Black Burn. Some took spades and forks and others just went along for a laugh, but none of them stayed for long. The rocks above stood ominous and silent. No one ever again saw a blue flame rise there, or heard a mysterious voice telling them where to dig for treasure. Something eerie seemed to emanate from the place and it unnerved folk. Eventually people stopped looking for buried gold at Carnduff, and as far as I know it has never been found again.

16

SITA, THE INDIAN PRINCESS OF LARKHALL

During the second half of the nineteenth century and early twen-tieth century, it was common for female domestic servants to be brought from India to Britain by their employers. They generally worked as housemaids and nannies, and were known as ayahs.

At least three high-ranking British military men appear to have brought back their Indian maids from the Boer War army camps in South Africa to live in their Lanarkshire homes. Very little is known about these women, who have become known locally as 'Black Ladies', their memory preserved through mysterious sightings and ghost stories.

Lesmahagow has a 'Black Lady' associated with Auchlochan House (the house and grounds now part of a retirement village) in South Lanarkshire. Her name is not recorded, but she was married to Major Douglas, who owned Auchlochan. It is rumoured that the Major's family would not accept her, or the marriage, and he was disinherited. She was seen as a great oddity to Scottish people of the day and not accepted socially. She lived out her life at the house, coming out to walk in the grounds only at night.

The Black Lady of Larkhall was Captain MacNeill's maid and she travelled to Britain on the same ship as another Indian maid,

who was taken to the home of Colonel Buchanan in Cambuslang.
These two women were not as lucky as the Black Lady of
Lesmahagow, they both disappeared separately and mysteriously.
This is the story of the Black Lady of Larkhall.

Down in the Avon Gorge, near to the Applebank Inn, just
below the town of Larkhall, the ghost of a beautiful Indian
woman is sometimes seen. Local tales say that a pungent aroma
of Asian spices fills the air when her spirit appears, and an overwhelming sense of grief accompanies this apparition. Her ghost
is known locally as the Black Lady.

This is the story of Sita Phurdeen, a beautiful Maharajah's
daughter, who came to live in Lanarkshire in 1902. Sadly, this
is not a fortunate tale of adventure, travel and loving racial inte-
gration, but rather a haunting story of enslavement, prejudice
and murder.

She was born in the Crown Colony of Ceylon (now Sri
Lanka) in 1862. Her religion was likely to have been Hindu-
Buddhist, and her family of high caste. Little is known of
Sita's early life, or what circumstances led her family to sell her
to a South African mining company. The practice of selling
daughters into servitude was not uncommon at this time in
India. As a young woman, Sita would have worked in the
mines, or been used for sex by a mine manager or overseer.
From there, she was then sold to the British Army, to serve
in their camps during the Boer War. Sita was a very attractive
woman, which meant she would most definitely have been
a sexual slave to higher-ranking officers in the army camp.
This is how she came to meet Captain Henry Montgomery
MacNeill Hamilton of Lanarkshire. MacNeill enjoyed Sita's
company enough to make sure that when the war was over,
she was freed from the camp. Both Sita and another Indian
camp maid accompanied Captain MacNeill and Colonel Gray
Buchanan on board the ship that took them back to Scotland.

Buchanan took his Indian servant home to his Lanarkshire estate at Cambuslang, and MacNeill took Sita to Broomhill House in Millheugh.

Here, Sita was kept secluded from MacNeill's family life and given work as a house servant, but rumour spread that she was his mistress. Lady Edith Hamilton, MacNeill's wife, had raised four children in Broomhill House with her husband, but it was not a happy marriage. MacNeill had a vicious temper – local villagers told stories of him riding his black horse at reckless speed along the paths and byways. He refused to slow down for anyone else using the path, or lane, and many were mown down, injured and even killed. One local miner recounted how when he was a lad, he'd climbed over the wall at the 'big hoose' at Millheugh, and been caught by the laird. A furious MacNeill aimed his whip at the child, slicing off the tops of three of the terrified boy's fingers.

The combination of MacNeill's affair with Sita, his brutality and bitter temper, plus Edith Hamilton's own ill health – she was suffering with tuberculosis – meant that it came as no surprise when Edith and the children left him and their home in 1910.

Sita's life at Broomhill House was clearly no happier than his wife's. One of her only comforts was to go walking, by herself, through the leafy gorge of Morgan Glen, on sunny days. Local folk remembered seeing her on the bridge below the house, watching the salmon leaping in the River Avon. These occasional sightings of a Maharajah's daughter always caused a great stir locally and set tongues wagging. Sita liked to mix her dress styles, teaming up silk sari trousers from her homeland with the Victorian vogue of crisply starched, embroidered blouses and tailored woollen jackets. All who met her were struck by her exquisite Asian beauty, her tall frame and unusual dress sense. Gentry and ordinary folk alike gazed, mouths open, at her exceptional high cheekbones, full lips and Kohl-lined, brown eyes. As she walked the country paths through Milheugh, the

smell of Eastern spices suffused the air around her; pungent
garlic, anise, cloves and cinnamon. She was in the habit of
chewing cardamom pods and spitting out the masticated pulp
at the side of the path. This was just too much for the local
people, who found her foreignness and exotic ways beyond
comprehension. Sita didn't fit in with MacNeill Hamilton's
upper-class cronies either. The lords and ladies of Scotland's
ruling elite found her too unconventional and immodestly
worldly wise. Mostly, Sita was kept hidden away in a room for
MacNeill's pleasure.

Life became harder for everyone at Broomhill House when
MacNeill was eventually diagnosed with syphilis – a common
disease among the British military in India, spread via the
brothels where women like Sita were used as prostitutes and
blamed by the British for giving the men the disease! Ageing
rapidly, and more violent and unpredictable than ever,
MacNeill slipped into continuous rages and insanity. The
disease was killing him. Sita's life must have been unbearable.
Then one evening in 1912 she vanished. The housekeeper
reported seeing Sita leaving the dining room after dinner and
retiring to her room at ten o'clock. The next day, Sita was
gone, there was no trace of her, and she was never seen again.
Hamilton explained her disappearance by insisting she had
decided to go home and had gone to get the train in Larkhall.
But the carriage had not been out, no one saw Sita in Millheugh
or Larkhall that evening, and the last train had left at 9 p.m.
Strangely, the Indian servant maid that Buchanan had taken to
Cambuslang also disappeared that same year. Sadly, there was
no one to report either of their disappearances and no one who
cared enough about the Asian maids to look for them.

Did Sita and her friend escape the life of servitude and
sexual exploitation by these perverse, damaged British military men? Many local people think not, because of the ghostly
sightings around where the house stood, and along the leafy

walkways of the Glen. After MacNeill died, aged fifty-two, the house was never lived in again by his family. Locals would occasionally go ghost hunting there. One tale described how Sita's ghost comforted a young lady who had fallen and hurt her leg inside the ruins of Broomhill House. Some reported smelling an overwhelming odour of spices, then the apparition of a tall, dark lady going past them in the night. Everyone who has witnessed her presence describes a sense of deep sadness and helplessness when she looks at them. Many clairvoyants and psychic researchers have investigated the area, variously reporting undiscovered corpses, murders, satanic practice and more than one ghostly presence. Their experiences suggest that far more nefarious deeds have taken place at the site of Broomhill House, going back many centuries before MacNeill and Sita's time. Helen, a Larkhall woman and the granddaughter of the housekeeper who last saw Sita alive, was particularly affected by a series of startling dreams that left her in no doubt that the Indian servant was murdered by the sick Captain MacNeill. It was Helen's research that revealed who Sita was, where she had come from and how she arrived at Broomhill House.

In the 1960s, the BBC made a programme about these disturbing hauntings, but unfortunately the director was killed in a car crash on his way home from the day's shoot in Larkhall!

A great sandstone lintel salvaged from the house was carried down to the Applebank Inn, situated in what's left of the old village of Millheugh. It took five men to carry it there because of its size and weight. The next morning, however, the block of stone was lying in the middle of the road. A local ghost researcher even claims that this lintel was the cause of his broken back. If you ever fancy going to see it for yourself, it is now part of the Applebank Inn, and you might also enjoy a stroll along the river, to watch the salmon leap.

When I first visited Morgan Glen, as a storyteller, a gorgeous big black cat strolled across the road in front of me. It paused and blinked at me, then carried on walking away from where Broomhill House had once stood. I've always believed that a black cat crossing your path is a sign of good luck, I blinked back at the cat. When I later discovered the story of the ghost of the Black Lady, I remembered the cat, and thought of beautiful Sita Phurdeen – after all, she was probably brought up as a Hindu-Buddhist and reincarnation is most definitely part of Buddhist and Hindu beliefs, isn't it!

17

THE CADZOW OAKS

In Chatelherault Country Park, near to the town of Hamilton, South Lanarkshire, there is a plantation of oak trees that date back to the Battle of Bannockburn in 1314. These trees are known as the Cadzow Oaks. They are part of the Clyde Valley Woodlands National Nature Reserve and are a remnant of the most ancient surviving oak woodland in Scotland. The oaks' saproxylic fauna supports insects and spiders like the rove beetle and cobweb beetle, which have become extremely rare.

Author Ian Hamilton QC, one of the Scottish students who liberated the Stone of Destiny from under the Throne of England at Westminster Abbey in the 1950s, says: 'This story was handed down to me by my father, who took me to see the Cadzow Oaks. The account was confirmed to me with a chuckle by Angus the last Duke, now dead. We flew his aeroplane together.'

This is the story of why the trees were planted.

Under the command of Robert the Bruce, the Scots fought the English army and defeated them at the Battle of Bannockburn in 1314.

Realising that he had been beaten, King Edward II of England fled from the battleground to save himself from being taken prisoner by the victorious Scots. Edward and a few of his men headed east to Dunbar, while many other English knights

fled to the south. Edward still held vital castles and strongholds
on the main routes to the English border. One such garrison
was the magnificent red sandstone castle at Bothwell. Many of
Edward's soldiers, knowing that the castle was still in English
hands, arrived here hoping to save their own lives and then,
God willing, regroup with their king in the future.

Walter fitz Alan de Hambleton and his son, Alan fitz Walter,
the two Norman knights in charge of Bothwell Castle, were in
a state of complete panic. With Edward's army defeated, they
knew that Bothwell would be a prime target for the Bruce, and
being cut off in a hostile country was a disastrous position to
be in for the two Englishmen. So, father and son decided to
switch allegiances. As each of Edward's fleeing soldiers galloped
into Bothwell, their weapons and armour were stripped from
them and they were promptly shown to an awaiting dungeon.
Horses, armour and weaponry were a very important source
of fluid wealth at this time and a knight's ransom was worth
a fortune. The Englishmen knew that the victorious Scottish
army would eventually arrive on their doorstep to capture back
the castle.

Sure enough, Robert's brother Edward Bruce and his men
arrived. Fitz Alan and fitz Walter, who were from the little town
of Hambleton in Northumberland, nevertheless opened the
drawbridge and welcomed Robert's victorious captains. They
offered the Bruce family their support, the castle and all of the
captured English soldiers. In return, the father and son were
hoping that the Bruce would then offer them the continuing
occupation and command of Bothwell Castle.

After Robert Bruce was consulted about what to do with fitz
Alan and his son, he thought carefully – being a great strate-
gist, he knew that as allies, two trained soldiers of their rank
were worth more as friends than as enemies. But Bruce was no
fool, these English soldiers had turned their allegiance once and
could turn again, so instead of Bothwell Castle, he offered them

the smaller Cadzow Castle and Barony. The castle and lands had been forfeited to the Scottish crown when the Comyn family, who had previously occupied Cadzow, had gone over to the English, and the Bruce needed a new landlord with army skills and a strong reason to be faithful to him and the Scottish cause. Still, cautious of the turncoats, Robert offered them only a short lease; for the time it took to grow and harvest one crop. The Bruce was pleased with this solution, it would repay the Englishmen for their peaceful surrender of Bothwell garrison to him and give everyone a year to see if their new role as soldiers for the Scottish army was tenable.

Fitz Alan and fitz Walter had no desire to go back to England after their treachery to Edward II. As they made their way to view Cadzow Castle, they were struck by the natural beauty of the surrounding Avon and Clyde Valleys and how lush the pasture land of Cadzow grew. White longhorn cattle grazed the meadows to the west of the castle and the crystal clear waters of the River Avon cascaded through the gorge below. Father and son knew that this fertile Scottish river valley, with abundant woodlands and strategically placed castle, was the best offer they were ever likely to get from the Scottish King. But the burning question, 'What crop to plant here for their tenure?' was the foremost thought in their minds. They surveyed the castle and land in great detail, pausing to drink from a flagon and rest under the sheltering branches of a sturdy oak tree. As his son discussed planting slow-growing wheat, turnips, oats or barley, fitz Alan looked up through the leaves and twigs of the majestic tree – perhaps for divine inspiration. His gaze pierced through the leafy canopy to the cloud formations in the sky, which were stacked like a staircase of eiderdown pillows leading upwards to heaven. A longhorn cow bellowed to her calf across the fields, two thrushes squabbled on a bough over the tree's bright-shelled crop of acorns, and wild pigs grunted and snuffled through the undergrowth on the small hillock where the men sat contemplating their future. Fitz Alan almost choked as he gasped in excitement at the thought that flashed through his mind.

'The acorns boy! The tree's fruit is the crop that feeds the birds, the boar, deer, squirrels, and the local people. This is the crop we must plant, Walter, acorns! We shall grow oak trees!'

Fitz Walter's mouth opened and closed, but no sound emerged, as he tried to grasp the genius of his father's suggestion. Eventually, he howled in celebratory joy.

'ACORNS! Darned right Father, we shall plant a crop of oaks. You sir, are without a doubt the wisest man I have ever met.'

His father smiled in satisfaction. 'Our one crop will still be maturing when you and I have long since passed on to meet our maker. This is the plant that will sustain the Hambletons for many generations to come.'

The men embraced and jigged around the oak tree in delight at their smart solution. Here was a place where they could settle and build a life for their family, a life fit for noblemen like themselves. They filled their pockets, leather pouches and caps with the acorns that were scattered about the tree's roots.

When the two wily Englishmen sent servants on to the land to plant a crop of oaks, the news of their clever strategy spread quickly. In due course, Robert the Bruce was consulted and, thanks to his finely honed wit, he appreciated the humour in the situation and recognised fitz Alan's intelligent choice. Bruce wanted his country secured and though he would always be cautious

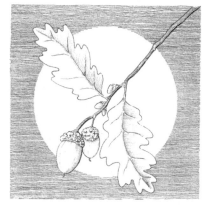

of turncoats, he felt that they were no threat to him while his courageous captain and strong ally, James Douglas, owned and controlled his estates to the south of Cadzow. There would be no fear of treachery while Douglas was around.

The two soldiers were confirmed in the lands of Cadzow as long as the oaks still grew. So the Fitz Hambletons, whose name eventually became Hamilton, settled into their new home in the Castle and Barony of Cadzow and watched with great pleasure as the oak trees grew, slowly.

The Hamilton family prospered over the centuries, inter-marrying with every titled family in Scotland, including the royal Stewarts, until they were only 'a baby's breath away from the throne itself'. The Cadzow Oaks are still there for everyone to visit, magnificent, gnarled old trees, a living memory from the county's action-packed and dramatic past.

18

THE CURLING WARLOCK
OF MAINS CASTLE

In the town of East Kilbride, in Rowan Avenue, you will find Mains Castle, a fourteenth/fifteenth-century tower, sitting proudly behind its own mini loch (or lochan), which is now a water sports centre. The last laird to live here, in the late sixteenth century, was Alexander Lindsay of Dunrod. The Lindsays were powerful and rich landowners with a reputation for being involved in the 'dark arts'. The family is described in Lives of the Lindsay *as: 'The Lindsays of Dunrod, a wild and warlock race, flourished for centuries in power and affluence and their history is a dark and stormy one.'*

The family were directly descended from Sir James Lindsay, Robert the Bruce's accomplice in the murder of John Comyn. Perhaps it was because of Sir James' involvement in such a cold-blooded murder that it was believed that a curse followed the family.

Another branch of his family, the Lindsays of Covington Castle, near Thankerton in South Lanarkshire, were remembered locally in rhyme:

Wha rides sae fast down
Culter Brae
The Deil or a Lindsay

(Averil Stewart, Links of Clyde, *p. 56)*

The story that follows concerns Alexander Lindsay, who during his lifetime was the epitome of a 'wild warlock'.

Alexander Lindsay's family came from Dunrod Hill, near Greenock in Inverclyde, where their castle stood, though he preferred to live at their other castle, The Mains, in Kilbride. Here, there was easy access to everything he needed and to one of his favourite amenities, the boating pool. In wintertime, when the water froze, Lindsay enjoyed nothing more than to play curling on the ice. He lived a lavish lifestyle with four attendees to follow him everywhere and serve his every need. He gained a reputation around Kilbride for his cruel and violent temper. The men who accompanied him rode four huge black horses and were instructed to be brutal in their treatment of both animals and any peasants who got in their way. The ordinary folk of the parish tried to keep hidden whenever they saw or heard Lindsay and his men coming.

Crawford, a farm worker and tenant of Laird Lindsay, was not so lucky one chilly winter's day when he was hurrying home from market. Alexander and his men were playing a game of curls on the frozen loch. Being chilled through, the laird spotted Crawford scurrying around the edge of the ice rink, and called him over with the intention of sending him to fetch more whisky from the castle. Crawford was hard of hearing and the whistling noise of the icy wind whisked the laird's shout away off in the opposite direction. Crawford, unaware that he was being summoned, merely raised his cap politely to the gentlemen, and carried on as fast as he could towards his cottage. Outraged at this peasant's insolence, Lindsay sent two of his men after Crawford. Stunned by blows to his head, the poor commoner collapsed and was dragged bodily before Lindsay of Dunrod. Pleading for clemency, Crawford explained his deafness and apologised for any misunderstanding. The more Crawford begged for forgiveness, the more Dunrod seemed incensed with rage. He commanded his henchmen to cut a hole through the ice. A hunting knife was used to make incisions in the ice, then a curling stone was hammered into the fracture to knock the ice through. A neat, round circle of ice was removed from the frozen loch, leaving a dark hole of icy water from which trails of mist rose up like eerie steam. The innocent tenant was pushed, screaming, into the ice hole and held down mercilessly by brutal hands. Briefly his cries of anguish filled the air around The Mains. Servants at the castle stopped for a moment, with an uneasy sense that something terrible and wicked was happening. At the edge of the loch, a cold, hungry heron lifted its great wings and flew away, turning its back on the crime scene. Crawford's body quickly became lifeless and his corpse was left to freeze into the surrounding ice sheet of the curling rink. Lindsay kicked at the bag of wheat grain, which Crawford had been taking home to his wife, now scattered on the ice around the dead man's body. He sneered momentarily at the dead peasant, ordered one of his troop to go and fetch a warmed dram of whisky from the house and then Dunrod and his mercenaries returned to their game of curls upon the frozen lochan.

Crawford's murder was not an isolated incident, Laird Lindsay of Dunrod continued to cause fear wherever he went. Surrounded by his men on their powerful chargers – like the four riders of the apocalypse – he felt invincible and acted with increasing malevolence towards peasants and nobility alike. Lindsay became involved in a bitter feud between some of the minor nobility. After he shot and killed one of his foes, Alexander Leckie, from a farmhouse window at Hayton Hill, near Glasgow, the King himself decided to intervene. The King punished Lindsay by taking nearly all of his lands at Kilbride. Now Lindsay was forced to spend most of his time in Inverkip. The people of Kilbride were very relieved by this turn of fate, many agreed that it was divine retribution for the laird's evil deeds – especially for the heartless murder of poor Crawford.

Back at Dunrod Castle, Lindsay's fortune began to decline. Over the next twenty years his money and luck ran out. Rumours of a devil-worshipping coven led by head warlock Lindsay Dunrod were rife all over the district of Inverclyde. When Dunrod's vast inheritance was spent, his lands and friends gone, he turned to selling charms and telling sailors' fortunes along the docks of the Clyde. Claiming to have supernatural powers and to be in league with a powerful sect of witches from the Inverkip area, the 'Ballad of Auld Dunrod' tells us that he 'sold favourable winds and immunity from the Evil One, to Sea Captains and fishers of the Clyde Coast'. The Church eventually intervened, taking what remaining lands he had away from him, and banishing him from the area. Lindsay Dunrod, now homeless and penniless, returned to Kilbride, where he wandered the countryside begging for alms from the very people he had once treated so cruelly. He died alone in a farmer's barn, his ill-fated family's curse fulfilled.

19

TIBBIE, THE WITCH OF KIRKTONHOLME

The oldest part of East Kilbride, where this story comes from, is Kilbride Village. The origins of Kilbride probably date back to the very early Christian Church, as the name Kilbride comes from the fifth-century Celtic Irish Saint Bride, or Saint Brigid of Kildare (451–525 CE). St Bride was patroness of farm work and cattle, as well as protector of the home from fire and calamity – it is no wonder that the National Museum of Country Life, with its working farm, is at Kittochside, in East Kilbride. Even older are the ancient pagan beliefs in Bride or Brigit, goddess of hearth, fire, childbirth, smiths, poets, healers and inspiration. And there is plenty of archaeological evidence of pre-Christian settlements in and around the area.

In 1820, with the arrival of a post office, the town was given the prefix of 'East' to distinguish it from West Kilbride on the west coast. After the Second World War, the town began to grow rapidly, becoming one of Scotland's New Towns. Lots of dual carriageways, roundabouts and shopping centres dominate this now huge town, but the old village of Kilbride is an attractive conservation area and well worth a visit to enjoy the boutique shops, cafes and art centre.

The great hurricane of 1780, in this story, which lasted for a week, seems to correlate to the storm in the story about Maggie Ramsay, the Witch of Auld Airdrie.

Long ago, an elderly woman named Tibbie lived at Kirktonholme in Kilbride Village – the oldest part of East Kilbride. She was a lonely and often crabbit old soul. And there was good reason why Tibbie had few friends and a scowl on her face – everyone in the parish thought she was a witch. Because of this, village folk thought it best to keep out of her way. When the locals met with each other on market days, or at church on the Sabbath, they often moaned about what was ailing them, like lumbago and toothache, or grumbled about bad luck when hens weren't laying, milk was curdling and horses were going lame. Sometimes folk even went as far as suggesting their misfortune had been caused by 'that soor-faced, auld witch'. They were, of course, referring to Tibbie, but no one ever dared complain in person to her. People were too afraid of what she might do to them. Behind the old lady's back, whispers, rumours and stories about her were constantly in circulation.

Tibbie's neighbours believed that she belonged to a mysterious coven of witches. Some claimed to have seen a group of wild war-locks and witches, on moonlit nights, dancing at the Bogle's Brig. This bridge at Rosemound was a notorious place for supernatural shenanigans. It had been named after a wicked bogle so long ago that no one in the village could remember the story of the bogle or its origin. The honest, church-going parishioners wouldn't dare go near the Brig on a full moon, or at Halloween, for this was when they believed that Tibbie's coven practised their dark arts. Occasionally, farmers and labourers returning home from the pub late at night reported seeing strange satanic rituals, with black-robed figures dancing in circles around leaping flames. Some said they had heard unearthly chanting and pipe music being played by the Devil himself. Others claimed to have seen the witches cavorting around a fire of blue flames, Satan in their midst, conducting the dancers, his cloven hooves kicking sparks high in the air from the hot coals beneath him.

Despite Tibbie's reputation as a sorceress, with diabolical connections and uncanny powers, she still went to the market every week to buy her groceries. Presumably she left her black cat and broomstick at home and walked into the village just like any other older lady. If anyone met her in the street they did their best to avoid eye contact with her, fearful of being harmed by the evil eye. When a market trader sold produce to her and an interaction with the 'auld wifey' was unavoidable, they were extremely polite to Tibbie, fearful of the hexes and misfortune she might curse them with. Some thought that the 'auld witch' enjoyed her notoriety, proud of her power over the simple village folk. To keep in with her, she was given the creamiest milk, freshest eggs, crispest vegetables and plumpest fowl from the market. This pleased Tibbie immensely, but she knew that it came from their fear and not from any real respect for her, so she hid her pleasure on market days with a well-practised scowl. No one dared cross her or sell her anything but the best for fear of unholy retribution. That was until the great hurricane of 1780.

That autumn, the biggest storm in living memory swept the country, wreaking havoc in its path. Huge wooden barn doors at Roddinhead steading were torn from their hinges and lifted through the air, past the church to Markethill. One eyewitness declared the storm had 'licket the Righead Burn as dry as the palm of ma hand'! Meaning the wind had been so powerful that it had swept the water out of the burn, leaving the rocky riverbed exposed, while the fields and lanes were deluged with water.

After many days, the tempest subsided and the stunned community emerged from what was left of their damaged homes. Many had perished, their houses, families and livestock obliterated by the force of the hurricane. Those who survived nursed the injured and dying, pulled bodies from the wreckage and buried the dead. As the shocked survivors embarked on cleaning up and repairing Kilbride Village, a rumour began to spread that this was the Devil's work. Naturally, with nerves frayed and traumatised tongues wagging, it wasn't long before Tibbie was blamed for the tempest. The survivors reasoned that if this was the Devil's doing, then someone local must have helped him. The consensus was that Tibbie was his accomplice. Her house, untouched by the great winds, was still standing. If so many good churchgoers had perished in the storm, and the old witch was alive, then it must be her master, Satan, who had unleashed the hurricane on their parish with her help.

Word spread quickly through the devastated village and a meeting was called. A few bewildered women, angry men and a couple of worthies gathered at the cross to discuss the matter. Amidst a great deal of shouting and cursing, the crowd decided the witch must be punished for her evil deeds. Although the Witchcraft Act had been repealed more than forty years earlier, the people of the parish could think of no other explanation for such terrible bad luck to strike their community.

Solid, heavy wooden stocks were fetched from the local gaol. It took several men to carry them, as the crowd marched along the street towards Kirktonholme, where the old woman lived. The plan was to drag the witch from her house, fasten her legs into the wooden clamps, and leave her in the market square as punishment for her wickedness. The mob gathered outside her gate, some shouting crude taunts, others asking for God's protection from this Devil's accomplice.

Tibbie poked her head out of the door, glaring contemptuously at the vengeful locals congregated outside her house.

'You're a foul witch,' cried the Burnsand's blacksmith, shaking his huge fist at the old woman.

Incredulous at the scene before her and realising what they were planning to do, Tibbie grabbed a stout walking stick and waved it fiercely at the rabble. Instantaneously the crowd stopped their advance, for fear of what horror she might unleash on them with her staff. Tibbie slashed the air with her stick, while hissing a torrent of insults at the ignorant villagers. On hearing her curses, many folk lost their nerve, convinced that the auld wife could do them serious harm. Their mission to put the woman in stockades was quickly abandoned, and the frightened locals hurried back to the safety of their homes. Doors were bolted and Bibles placed by folk's chimneys to keep malevolent forces from flying 'doon their lums' (chimneys) and entering their homes.

Over the next few days and weeks the work continued around the parish to clear up the devastation caused by the hurricane. People still muttered and gossiped about Tibbie, convinced she had summoned the winds to bring misery to their community. Then a strange thing happened to one of the blacksmith's sheep. The events that unfolded were the final proof needed for anyone still not convinced of Tibbie's credentials as a witch.

A local man coming home from the inn reported that he saw Tibbie, wrapped in a black shawl, hopping over the fence into the fold where the blacksmith's flock were grazing. There he witnessed her standing over one animal, making strange movements with her bony hands. As he watched on, unseen and amazed, he heard her speaking odd words and chanting unearthly incantations. Then the bewitched beast leaped up in the air and began to twist and turn as if dancing reels and hornpipes. The crazed sheep bleated loudly, as it tumbled head over heel, rolling down the hillside all the way to the Kittoch Water, where it somersaulted into the river with an almighty splash. When the blacksmith later recovered the corpse of his ewe, it was clear that the animal had broken its neck.

Tibbie's revenge against the man who had dared to call her a 'witch' to her face left no one in any doubt of her allegiance with the Devil.

The parish minister of Kilbride Village, the Reverend David Connell, was well aware of the prejudices local folk had toward Tibbie. He also knew that the Church no longer believed in or persecuted people for witchcraft. However, when called out one dark night to perform an exorcism on a ghost that had been terrorising the town, he came to his own conclusions about the truth of the accusations against her. As he and his assistant, David Ure, were performing their religious ceremony to banish the ghost from the streets of old East Kilbride, a wild and unnatural wind swept over their heads. The two men looked up to see a swirl of dark cloud blasting eerily across the sky. There, within the vapours above them, was Tibbie surrounded by a dozen witches, all seated on broomsticks. The strange breeze swept the airborne coven east towards the Bogle's Brig, where they were, no doubt, going to join their diabolical gathering with Auld Nick himself.

There was one last sighting of Tibbie flying over Kilbride Village on her broom. It was reported to the minister that she was seen, on a bright moonlit night, to have flown over the church-yard and around the kirk, chanting and laughing as she cruised through the sky. Shortly after this she died, and no one could blame Tibbie the witch of Kirktonholme for raising storms, curdling milk, or bewitching sheep ever again.

20

THE TALE OF KATE DALRYMPLE

'Kate Dalrymple' was a poem and song written by William Watt (1792–1859), a handloom weaver from East Kilbride. Kate's poem appears in Songs Humorous and Sentimental, *published posthumously in 1860. This song is still popular with folk musicians in Scotland today.*

On the lonely moors of East Kilbride lived an older, unmarried woman called Katie Dalrymple. She lived alone with nothing but the cry of the peewit and the gurgle of the burn to listen to on long dark nights and solitary days. Kate could have walked into the village to gossip with the locals on market day, but she'd long ago grown tired of folks' sly smirks and cruel comments, so she kept herself to herself, as much as she possibly could. You see, poor Kate had not been blessed with what folk considered to be a bonny face – or even a common, plain face – and people were as shallow about a woman's looks back then as they are today! She'd inherited her long Roman nose from her father's side of the family – her grandfather always claimed his forbears had mingled with the Roman army that had built the Antonine wall across Scotland. Maybe that's why her sinuses pained her so much – the drip and sniffle in her nose was always bothered by the dreich Scottish weather. Her lazy eye and pimply skin came from her mother's side of the family, and goodness knows how one leg came to be shorter than the other, but that was definitely the reason for her limp.

Kate had never been asked out to the village fairs or to the dances by the local lads and no one had ever shown any interest in being her sweetheart. When all of her family had passed away, she'd been left to look after herself, alone in her wee cottage among the windswept heather. She may have never been lucky in love, or described as beautiful, but she certainly was a good worker. Kate grew all the food she needed in her garden during the spring, summer and autumn months. She cut peat from the moor for her fires, grew enough wheat and stacked her hayricks to see her through the winter, and spun wool all through the dark months to make enough money to live on.

One day, though, Katie's luck took a turn for the better. Her neighbour, a rich man who had always admired Katie's resilient character and finely spun wool, passed away and left his entire estate and riches to Kate. From that day on, she was never lonely again. The first to arrive at her door, on a fine-bred stallion, was a local laird. He presented her with a bouquet of roses from his gardens and tried to woo Katie over tea and cake. His flattering attentions did not impress her one bit, in fact she found the situa-tion very embarrassing. Next to come and try his luck was a lawyer from the town, followed by a provost, then a doctor. Katie had a long line of would-be suitors arriving to lavish gifts, compliments and smiles upon her. The doorbell to the cottage was rung daily by men, and a couple of women, hopeful to charm Miss Dalrymple with their flattery and gifts.

Katie turned them all down for she had a notion of her own. She finally plucked up the courage to visit the man she had always had a fondness for, Willie Speedyspool, the fastest weaver in the parish. Willie was shy, but when Katie made her feelings for him known, he was over the moon that she had chosen him. Willie had always secretly admired Kate, but because of his droopy right eye and bandy left leg, he had never dared to think that she might be able to love him back. Now, Willie wasted no time in proposing to his own dearest Katie. Kate Dalrymple said, 'Yes!' They were soon happily married and everyone agreed that they made a very fine and contented couple.

BARTRAM, THE GIANT OF SHOTTS

In the fourteenth century, the average height of a Scotsman was 5½ft (1.67m), so when a man named Bartram, or Bertram, grew to be 6ft 10in tall (2.08m) everyone thought of him and remembered him as being a giant. Through time, and the telling of his story, this giant of a man became known as Bartram de Shotts, in memory of the land he cultivated, and the place where he robbed the rich to feed the poor. The Kirk O'Shotts is a very prominent church standing alongside the M8 motorway as you enter North Lanarkshire, and St Katie's Well is still there – once famous for its fish-friendly water, especially for keeping pet fish in and curing sick fish.

Bartram grew up on Bothwell Muir, a windswept moorland in what is now part of North Lanarkshire. It was here that Bart toiled day and night to tame the rough heather and peat moor, cultivating enough land on which to grow food, so that he could survive. Few men or women even then – eight hundred years ago – would ever have attempted the huge amount of hard labour needed to make this poor soil and land productive but, of course, Bartram did have an advantage over most folk – he was a giant! The work was slow and back-breaking. However, Bartram had been brought up to love and respect wild places, the plants, trees and creatures, so he worked tirelessly to make the barren hillside his own fertile land. He put his enormous stature to great use, digging, tilling and sowing seed on the scrubland, until he had enough pasture for a few grazing animals and healthy soil for growing vegetables and crops.

Bordering Bartram's hillside was the road at Kirk O'Shotts, which led through the inhospitable glen. This road ran east to west across the county and was as important a highway then, in Bart's day, as it is today. Local tradesmen, tinkers and livestock herders, as well as travellers including wealthy nobles and merchants, used this route to take them to Glasgow, Edinburgh, everywhere in-between and to access the highways to the north and south.

Bartram would regularly encounter people on their journeys through the region. Most travellers would welcome the sight of his friendly face. Some would gasp, stop and stare, incredulous at his great height. Others would admire his tenacity, wondering at the relentless hardship of his agricultural labours in such a wild landscape. Local girls would blush and sneak coy glances at him. Big and bold as Bartie's frame was, his face was like that of an innocent boy with gentle eyes and a rosy, healthy complexion. His solitude and life on the savage moor, however, meant Bart had little time or understanding of grooming. His appearance was distinctly unkempt. With long, thick hair and a fox-red beard of coiled, wiry growth, he had a natural, animalistic beauty.

Bartram travelled weekly to the village market to buy and sell provisions. Depending on the season, he sold sheep fleeces, wild game, stoat and hare pelts, firewood, heather and his surplus vegetables. When he had made himself a little money, there was nothing he enjoyed more than visiting the local inn. Here he kept up to date with the news, socialising with the locals and especially with the landlady. He admired her auburn curls and generous smile, and the more ale she served him, the more inclined he was to let her know how fond he was of her.

After a couple of wet summers and even harsher winters, Bartram and all the folk who lived and made their livings from the land were suffering from terrible food shortages. He barely had enough kale in his yard to feed himself, let alone to trade or sell in the village. The poorest and oldest folk were always the hardest hit during difficult times. After hearing about a heartless landowner who had turned a poor old couple out of their cottage on his estate, leaving them homeless in the midst of the bitterly cold winter, Bartram's good nature snapped. He made a plan to teach the ruthless laird a lesson.

Hiding himself behind a blackthorn and bramble thicket halfway up the hillside, Bart waited for the laird to pass by on his horse on the road below. He took his bow and arrows and shot the passing man, wounding him severely in the shoulder. Then Bartram strode down the hill and robbed the injured nobleman of his money. With the silver stolen from the laird Bartram treated himself and many of the starving townsfolk to the food and grain they needed to keep themselves, their bairns and livestock alive that winter.

Maybe because of Bart's good humanitarian deed, or because of his great height and strength, perhaps even due to the lack of law enforcement at that time, nobody came to challenge him about the robbery. Bart felt a great sense of righteousness for his actions, satisfied that justice had been done. From that time on, the once inhumane, injured laird seemed to be less contemptuous of and more respectful to his tenants and workers. The local villagers whom Bart had helped now treated him as a hero. Each May Day, a group of travelling players came to enact the Robin Hood and His Merry Band play at the village celebrations, so everyone knew the story. Locals agreed that Bart was just like the famous Robin who stole from the rich to give to the poor.

Bartram enjoyed his new-found popularity, especially when visiting the market and the village inn. The weather, however, continued its deluge, devastating the land. Another harvest

failed. This caused terrible hardship and misery among the
ordinary people. As illness and starvation decimated his local
community, Bartram decided, once again, to shoot and rob
a wealthy traveller on the lonely road. He ambushed another
titled scoundrel with a reputation for cruelty and contempt
towards those less well off than himself. Leaving the man fatally
wounded on the lonely moor, Bartram confiscated his silver
and goods, and used the stolen money to help the local people.

This continued for several years. As long as there were needy
folk to feed and help, and as long as over-privileged merchants
and aristocrats travelled through Bartram's stretch of land, he
was ready to commit highway robbery and then redistribute the
ill-gotten wealth to those who needed it most.

Eventually, though, the infamy of the giant robber from the
village of Shotts spread far and wide and the King himself became
aware of the situation. When King Robert II's own cousin and
entourage were robbed near Kirk O'Shotts, the King decided that
something must be done to protect the wealthy from this barba-
rous giant of a man. Robert set a bounty on Bartram's head – a
'Hawks Flight of Land' to be given to the person brave enough to
take on this fearsome thief and deliver his head to the King.

William de Muirehead, a neighbouring laird and landowner
whom Bartram had shot at and stolen from on more than one
occasion, decided to take up the King's challenge. He knew the
area better than most and was familiar with the highway robber's
haunts and routines. For revenge on the commoner who had taken
his own silver and for the reward of land granted from the King
himself, Muirehead worked out a devious plan to ambush Bart.

William sent his men to cut and gather heather from the
moor and stack it in a tall bundle alongside the track that led to
St Katherine's Well.

The next day, Bartram passed exactly by the place where the
heather had been left. He always drank from this spring. It gave
the purest water of any well in Scotland, and he knew it would

keep him healthy till his dying day. When Bart saw the heather stacked high like a hayrick beside the path, he checked it curiously and poked his stick into the middle.

'Nothing to worry about,' he thought to himself. 'Just a cover for some local toff to hide himself in and shoot at the deer on the hillside.'

The next day, when Bartram passed by the track once more, he glanced at the rick of heather and thought no more of its presence than he would the docken plants growing about the hillside. He had toiled hard that day, so he stopped and sighed at the sound and sight of the bubbling spring. He laid his long lean body down over the tufts of coarse moor grass and dipped his chin and lips into the clear water. While Bartram lay flat on his belly drinking from the spring, Muirehead crept out of the heather hide, his broadsword gripped hard in his hands. Three of his men, camouflaged with spiky fronds of cut heather sticking out from their tunics and bonnets, followed cautiously behind.

Muirehead was upon Bartram in two strides, the giant still lay on the ground, his face in the spring water. Flashing quick as lightning, Muirehead brought the sword down in two sharp cuts to the giant's hamstrings. Bart screamed in pain and shock. He turned, twisting his torso to see his attacker. Blood gushed from the back of his thighs, Bart's legs almost cut in two. Searing pain made him almost fall into unconsciousness, but as his eyes fixed on William Muirehead and his approaching men, he realised the trap into which he had fallen. Bart twisted his head further, and looking Muirehead fully in the eye, he laughed out loud. Raising his fingers, dripping wet, from St Katie's spring water, he pointed to Muirehead's sword.

'Tis a keen, sharp sword you have in your hand there, Muirehead. I'll wager it's a sharper sword than mine, but 'tis far more treacherous a sword than I bear. For mine has only ever been drawn against a man to his face, with a sword in his hand, and never behind a man's back whose sword was not drawn.'

Bart groaned in agony, but catching his breath, he determined to keep his focus on his assassin.

'I'll no bother to ask for mercy Muirehead, for I see 'tis not in your weak and cowardly soul.' As Bartram uttered these defiant words to the trembling laird and his scoffing helpers, he let out a laugh of pure scorn and pity at the dastardly laird.

William was beside himself with fury at Bartram's arrogance and, drawing his broadsword up once more, he swore by Saint Katie.

'Look up and lauch at me would you?! Well it will be the last look and lauch you ever give, you scoundrel!'

With these words, Muirhead brought his mighty sword down on Bartram's neck, severing his head from his body.

When the giant's head was delivered to the King in Edinburgh, Robert II was delighted that another commoner with ideas beyond his birthright had been dispatched satisfactorily. True to his word, Robert had a hawk sent to Lanarkshire, which was set free to fly around the moor. Its flight was recorded, and the land it had flown over was given to William de Muirhead.

In memory of Bartram, the dying man brave enough to 'lauch up' in the laird's face, the land is still known to this day as Laudehope (Laugh Hope).

22

THE WHITE HARE

The Scottish mountain hare's fur turns white in the winter months to help it blend into its snowy surroundings. The brown hare, however, which is much more common in the Scottish Lowlands, does not go through this colour transformation and remains brown all year round. All hares, whether white (Lepus timidus) or brown (Lepus europaeus), have long been associated throughout the world with fertility, the moon, magic and witches.

This old Monklands legend is rich in the superstitious beliefs of the sixteenth century in which a witch could shape-shift into an animal. The story combines a tragic family curse with Scotland's favourite witch's familiar, the hare.

After the Reformation in Scotland in 1560, times were difficult for ordinary and rich folk alike. Lord Ronald Ker, a Protestant and staunch supporter of the Hanoverian cause, moved to the Monklands Estate, a quiet and sleepy backwater in those days. Here he could avoid the turmoil of town, city and political life and keep his only child, Lady Janet – known affectionately as Jennie – away from young Lord Charles Hope, her would-be lover. Charles supported the Stuarts and Lord Ker was determined that no romance would develop between his daughter and this man, his Catholic enemy.

Little did the father and widower Ronald know that a romance was indeed already flourishing between Jennie and Charles.

The two young lovers had met at a ball in Edinburgh. It was quite literally love at first sight, and after an evening of dancing together, the couple had no intention of looking any further for a sweetheart. With a father and potential son-in-law so diametrically opposed in religious and political views, Lady Janet and Lord Charles had conducted their affair, for many moons, through an exchange of love letters and clandestine rendezvous. Jennie's faithful maid, Girzie, had helped set up secret meetings for the couple and delivery of scented notes, with passionate poetry and sweet declarations of undying love for each other. In fact, it was Girzie who was to play the main role in helping her love-smitten mistress elope with her young man.

After dinner one dark January evening, Jennie, who had eaten very little, made her excuse to retire early to her room. She kissed her father goodnight and asked her maid servant to clear away the dinner dishes quickly, so she could bring her a stone pig, filled with hot water, to warm her bedsheets before bedtime.

Her father approved the task given to the maid, it was a very chill evening. He poured himself a mulled port from the hearth pan at his fireside, while maid and daughter flitted out of the dining room. As he passed the window of the grand room, Lord Ker stopped in shock. There, through the glass, he saw a white hare making its way slowly and deliberately across the garden lawn below. The creature paused for a second or two and seemed to look straight up at the man standing, mouth open, in the window of the great house. Ker closed the heavy velvet curtains to block the sight of the animal. This was a very bad omen for the man and his family. He staggered slightly and slumped down hard in his chair, spilling hot port down his breeches. He knew only too well the old family prophesy and muttered it quietly, as if telling it to the spitting logs in the fire grate, 'A white hare is wae for Ker.' This had been passed from one generation of his family to the next, the origin of it lost somewhere back among his ancestors. The meaning was clear though: seeing a white hare spelled disaster for his kin.

Upstairs in Janet's bedroom, the maid and excited young woman were hastily putting the rest of the few belongings Janet planned to take on her elopement into a saddle bag. Jennie, looked nervously out of her window, it was almost time to leave and meet her lover at the agreed place. Jennie gasped and clutched at her curtain. 'Girzie, look on the grass … a hare, a white hare!'

Lady Janet knew the family curse too and here was the omen of ill luck, staring back up at her.

The maid looked out and drew the curtains shut sharply. Quick as anything, she reassured her mistress that hares strayed down south during the cold winter months and there was nothing unusual about seeing it tonight. Girzie knew the family's omen of seeing a white hare and bad luck following, but she was practical and knew the young lord would be waiting. She persuaded Lady Janet to stay calm and courageous and meet her lover as planned.

The two women, wrapped warmly in woollen coats and furs, slipped out of the servants' door quieter than mice. They flitted like ghosts around the stable yard and out through the side entrance towards the Calder Brig. There, a figure of a slender man with a fine horse moved from the shadows and into their path. Charles and Jennie embraced fervently. Girzie kissed her dear mistress goodbye through tears of love and sadness, passing up her lady's satchel of treasured possessions, as Charles lifted her up behind him on to his horse. The couple galloped away down the road, towards their life of joy and freedom together. As they sped round the curve in the road, out of sight of Girzie and the house, a flash of white darted out from the verge. The hare sprang between the horse's hooves and the animal reared up in fright. The startled horse bolted down the glen and leaped across the ravine above the Calder Water. The terrified beast never had a chance to clear the span across the chasm, and down they all plummeted.

The next day, a search party found the lifeless
bodies of Lady Janet and Lord Charles, entwined
in an embrace of broken limbs, entombed in the
gorge. Strangely, the horse was never found.
From that day on, the spot in
Monklands Gorge was
known as the Lovers
Loup (Lovers Leap).

On the same
morning that the lovers'
bodies were discovered
in the glen, the tenant
of Faskine Toll House
was woken by his wife
groaning in agony with
a sore foot. When they
arose and looked at her
injury, it appeared to be
broken with the imprint of
a horse's hoof across it. The
confused and upset
woman was made
to swear on the
Holy Bible before
the Minister and two
Elders that she had never left her bed on the previous evening.
From that day on she was known as Horse-Shoe Jean and locals
gave her a wide berth at Kirk and Market on account of the
sinister association with that fateful night when a white hare
had appeared to Lord Ker and Lady Janet in Monklands Glen.

23

MAGGIE RAMSAY: THE WITCH OF AULD AIRDRIE

In the eighteenth century, the North Burn in Airdrie, in the parish of New Monkland, was known to be haunted by the ghost of a witch called Maggie Ramsay. Many believed that Maggie was haunting the area even before she died. These are a few of the stories that people told about her.

Maggie and her husband Tam had spent an enjoyable day at Airdrie Fair, followed by a fun evening at a penny reel in East High Street. On their way home to their little house in Rawyards, they were unlucky enough to run into a press gang. These were tough guys employed by the government to find suitable men to serve in the King's Navy. The paid thugs waited outside taverns and bars, grabbing men who were the worse for wear through alcohol. When they spotted Tam he was too tipsy after his day and night out to make a run for it or to put up a fight. Maggie screamed and hit out at them with all of her strength, but a huge, scary member of the crew, with a scar that split his face down the middle, threatened her with an iron bar. She stopped her attack on the men, fearing for both their lives. Tam was restrained by two big bruisers, who threw him into a covered wagon. Here were many other sorry-looking souls who'd been abducted in the same way. Some of the lads were bloodied and bruised and a couple of them either unconscious through drink or from the brute force the press gang had used to snatch them off the street. There was nothing more Maggie or Tam could do, this was how the British Navy recruited sailors to serve at sea for King and country. As the cart was driven down the street and out of view, Maggie wailed in despair, collapsing to the ground, her world shattered.

From that day on, left on her own, Maggie struggled to cope. Neighbours and townsfolk noticed that she was spending most of her time wandering upon Airdrie Hill, which on a clear day is visible from the North Sea. Maggie seemed to be scanning the horizon constantly, muttering to herself, trying to get a glimpse of her Tam's ship. Folk reckoned she was so stressed by the shock and grief of losing Tam that her behaviour was becoming more and more unhinged.

Maggie finally gave up looking for ships from the hill and turned her attention to her knowledge of herbs and plants. She had to find a way to make a living now that she didn't have her man to provide for her. So she put her understanding of plant-lore to good use and became a Spey-wife, providing herbal cures, charms and potions to local folk. At first, it was mostly country lads and lasses who came to her, wanting to know how to attract a lover, and who they might marry. She would sell them a little bag of fragrant rose petals and verbena. The hopeful youngsters put the posies of herbs under their pillow at night, trusting that they would dream of their future partner. Maggie was often seen walking the length of the burn, collecting plants by the different quarters of the moon, and at varying times of day and night, according to the hours of plant potency. This herb craft she learned from a great almanac. People reported that they heard her talking to herself as she went about her business, and some even suggested that she was speaking to an unseen companion.

She read palms and tea leaves too, earning herself a reputation as far as Glasgow for her skills in predicting the future. News of Maggie's fortune-telling spread fast and wide. This, however, had an unpleasant consequence, for the Church delivered her a censure, ordering Maggie to give up her 'nefarious practices'. She ignored the kirk's warnings and refused to obey the minister, continuing her trade in cures and predictions. This made matters worse and the Church pronounced the ban of lesser excommunication on Maggie. This forbade the parishioners of New Monkland to have any further dealings with her. Now people really began to gossip about Maggie Ramsay and the stories grew more far-fetched and shocking than before.

Maggie was an expert field worker and her services were always in great demand, especially during harvest time. Even with the Church's excommunication hanging over her, local farmers still hired her, on the quiet, to reap their corn fields. When one such farmer, Johnstone of Bogend Farm, had spent the day reaping his fields with her, they had a violent quarrel about how much he would pay for the work. Bogend ended up calling her a second 'Witch of Endor' (a witch from the Bible). Maggie responded by warning him that if he didn't watch what he said about her, he'd end up regretting his words. Within a fortnight of this heated exchange one of his cows died, his family all became ill with a mysterious disease, and his sheep – and his alone – were worried by an unknown dog. There was no doubt whatsoever among the local folk that Maggie Ramsay was now far more sinister than a simple Spey-wife, she was, in their minds, definitely a witch. Many stories proliferated about her cunning deeds and the Devil himself began to make appearances in the tales told about her, after all, who was the invisible companion she was heard talking to as she harvested the hedgerows for berries and wild plants?

One such story was very popular with local people. Told around the hearth on windy winter nights, or when the wild fire (Aurora Borealis) was dancing in the northern sky. It is known locally as 'When the De'il Helpit Wi' Airdrie's Haurvest' and is worth retelling.

WHEN THE DEVIL HELPED WITH AIRDRIE'S HARVEST

One autumn, when a band of Highland shearers and reapers were travelling through the Monklands district looking for work, an old farmer, Rab Allan, hired them to help with his harvest. On the first night, Rab took them down to the inn at Burnhouse and together they sat blethering over pints and drams of whisky. The head of the group, Left-Handed Sandy, was a champion reaper and after a few more drams he began recounting stories from all the places he and the boys had travelled for work. Sandy was reputed to have the second sight, so his stories had a supernatural tinge to them, but the more he drank, the more boastful he became about his own reaping skills. Never one to miss a chance, Rab cannily announced that he had 'a woman who could reap twice as much in one day as Sandy ever could!' Insulted at the thought of a woman ever being considered better than him at his job, Sandy accepted the challenge and a reaping contest was agreed for the following day.

Auld Rab greeted Left-Handed Sandy and the Highlanders the next day and showed them where they were all to work. He took Sandy into the middle of his largest field and introduced him to his opponent, who was none other than Maggie Ramsay. The two began their work from the centre of the barley, outwards in opposite directions. After an hour or two of hard work, Sandy straightened up and stretched his back and took a quick look to see how his competitor was doing. He was amazed to see that Maggie had not only covered twice the distance he had, but she had 'stooked' her work as well. What surprised him even more was that she was not alone. A man appeared to be working alongside her, doing the reaping, while Maggie constructed the stooks of barley.

Feeling cheated, Sandy stormed over to the man helping Maggie and challenged him, but the man just ignored Sandy's indignant protests and carried on at his work.

'You'll not double cross me you scoundrel,' Sandy said as he took a swipe at the fella with the side of his hook. To his surprise, the hook passed clean through the silent reaper. Sandy swung again at him, making sure he aimed carefully, but once again his tool swished straight through, as though the man was only an apparition and not flesh and blood. Once more, Sandy tried to knock the stranger with his reaping hook, aiming low at the legs. To Sandy's horror, he saw that the legs ended in two cloven hooves. Realising now who Maggie's colleague was, a terrified Sandy ran screaming to his friends.

When he told them that Maggie was being helped by the Devil himself, they laughed at him. He persuaded a couple of his compatriots to come and see for themselves, but as they had not been blessed with the second sight, they saw only a lone woman methodically stacking and stooking her work. Sandy did not stay around long enough to pick up his wages, but hastily left Monklands to find work in a more godly community.

Auld Rab, delighted at the speed his big field was harvested, made sure everyone was treated to an extra dram of whisky that night, and the highland men were amused that Sandy had been beaten by a woman. Now they hoped he'd be less inclined to boast about his reaping skills when they gathered for a pint or two together.

Not all of the stories told about Maggie were so sinister. For instance, one tale concerned Rab Mair, who went out one day to take stock of his sheep, pastured out near New Monkland. Not being in any great hurry to get the job done, he dropped into Wull Aitken's for a dram and a 'crack'. When he was well refreshed, he carried on his way but could not resist having a taunt at Maggie, who was out working in a field, along the road. She merely looked at him, then turned around widdershins (anticlockwise) and carried on with her work. Rab stoated on along the road until he reached the field, where his sheep were grazing contentedly. Try as he might, Rab could not make an accurate tally of his sheep. Each time he counted the beasts, he either ended up with far too many in number than he actually had, or far too few. Convinced that Maggie had bewitched him and befuddled his brains with her glance, he hurried back to Wull Aitken's. Here Wull made sure that Rab was cleansed from the effect of the evil eye, out of the same whisky bottle he had drunk from earlier that day.

Not long after this incident, fortunately for Maggie, Tam Ramsay returned from serving in the King's Navy. He'd lost half a leg, but had gained a small pension. Finding the neighbourhood gossip about Maggie and her exploits with the Devil a little too uncomfortable, the couple moved to a cottage on the Dunsyston Road. Here they concentrated on a small business rearing poultry and eggs, which did well in Airdrie's growing, industrious population. Every Saturday, they took their produce to market, baskets of eggs and plucked fowl. When all were sold and the week's provisions bought, Tam, Maggie and their big black dog, called Darkie, would stroll arm in arm to Wull Main's Inn for a quick refreshment, then home, the dog proudly carrying the message basket in its mouth. They became devoted attenders of Bertram Shotts Kirk, although Maggie refused to take Communion. Tam was a striking figure, wearing his navy reefer jacket, with brass buttons, gold-braided cap and his pin leg, which earned him the nickname 'Captain'.

A few years passed quietly and Maggie and Tam seemed happy and contented together. One year, towards the end of March, a terrible storm raged over Monklands, lasting over a week and causing havoc and destruction everywhere. When the winds had abated and people began to clear away the debris, it was discovered that Tam and Maggie's wee cottage had been completely destroyed. Tam's dead body was found in the wreckage, but there was no trace of Maggie or the dog. It was later in the month that some boys off to guddle for fish in the North Burn made a frightening discovery. Seated on a big rock at the side of the burn was a woman with long hair, guarded by a huge black dog. As the boys approached to get a better look, the dog snarled and growled at them menacingly. Frightened, the boys ran home and told their parents. A party was gathered and the kirk minister, Pate Tamson, came with them for holy protection. The boys' story was verified, as there where they had described was indeed a woman; however, the dog had vanished. On closer inspection they found that the woman was dead and it was none other than the infamous Maggie Ramsay. As it was a Sunday, it wasn't till the following day that the proper authorities went to recover the body, but when they arrived it had gone and nothing but a few long strands of grey hair were found attached to a sapling tree, behind the rock. How Maggie's body had ended up down at the Auld North Burn was never explained, well not by rational thought, at least.

The large square rock in the burn was known as Maggie's Chair, or the Witch's Chair, from then on. Many stories were told to scare children of how she sat on the rock to wash her hair with a ferocious devil dog by her side. The red-eyed dog would chase anyone who dared to come near into the water and drown them. The place had been associated with witches long before Maggie's time. The meadow on one side being called Fiddlenaked, as local folk once believed that witches came here to dance naked with the Devil. It was described as covered in woodbine (honeysuckle) and briar roses. The Virtue Well, near the burn (now filled in), was a place of pilgrimage to poor folk looking to cure TB and skin diseases. The mineral-rich waters and healing plants that grew around the burn must have been known to herb-wives, charmers and healers for many centuries; Maggie Ramsay being just one in a long tradition of folk who used natural remedies as a healing art.

Following Maggie's death, people thought that she had laid a curse on the North Burn and anyone who misused the water would meet a dreadful end. It is no surprise to hear that the chap who many years later dynamited Maggie's rock and used the stone for road building was said to have drunk himself to death.

THE LOWER WARD

24

THE RUTHERGLEN BANNOCK

This tale from Rutherglen, which is the northernmost town in South Lanarkshire, forming the boundary with Glasgow, is about an annual harvest rite where the women of the community made sour, or soul, cakes – special sacramental bannocks – for Saint Luke's Fair, which was held on 18 October on the site of Rutherglen Old Parish Church. There has been a church here since the sixth century, built by St Conval, a disciple of St Kentigern, Glasgow's patron saint. However, evidence of an ancient ring of trees found around the grounds of the church suggest that it may have been a sacred Druids grove and pagan site of worship long before the first Christian church was built here. This story describes the ritual of how these Halloween bannocks were made.

Every autumn, the people of Rutherglen looked forward to the special evening when they were invited to the Soul Cake Ceremony. How long this event had been taking place, nobody knew – the origins of the custom were lost in time. From mother to daughter, the ritual had been passed down through countless generations. Since they were bairns, the women of the community had watched their grandmothers, mothers and older sisters make and toast the bannocks for Saint Luke's Fair.

Agnes's farm was a mile south of Main Street in Rutherglen. The village had grown steadily over the years, and weavers' cottages and dirt roads now occupied what was once farmland. From the centre of the wee town it was an easy trek, along an even track, to Agnes and Jock's farm. Her kitchen was a decent size and this year, like many before, Agnes's house was chosen for the Soul Cake Celebration.

The women, mostly related by birth or through marriage, arrived early. They spent a convivial afternoon making the dough for the cakes. Agnes put plenty of sugar and cinnamon into the mix, to make sure that they were sweeter and tastier than any other cakes in the whole of the parish. Jock did his best to keep out of their way, while tending the fire and keeping the kettle filled. A delicious perfume of spice and aniseed rose from the sticky dough, as it sat in an earthenware bowl placed in a pan of warmed water to help it rise gently, while outside the daylight faded.

At sunset, Jock was stationed at the door to welcome his neighbours and friends. Settles and stools had been moved from the kitchen into the vestibule and hall and onlookers began squeezing in, ready to enjoy the fun of the occasion.

Earlier that afternoon, Jock had mixed a little lime and flour with water, and now, with the edge of a stiff barn brush, he carefully painted a thick white line in a circle on the kitchen's flagstone floor.

A burst of excited laughter and giggles broke out from the pantry, where the eight cake-makers were hiding, busily fixing their hair and tidying their aprons, in readiness for the ceremony to begin. Composing themselves, the women filed, one at a time, into the kitchen, singing an old song about harvesting the oats and wheat to make bannocks. The youngest, Katharine, was still in her teens. She sat down closest to the fire on the east side of the room, and the other girls and women took their place around the circle, ending with Agnes, the elder of the baking team, who stood next to the fire on the western side of the hearth.

Jock watched closely, as Agnes raised her hand and summoned him to bring a stack of baking boards forward. Each of the bakers, except Agnes, was handed a large, smoothed piece of elm wood on which to work her baking magic. Poor old Jock fumbled while giving out the equipment and as he tried to grab a baking board that was slipping out of his grip, he accidentally staggered into the consecrated circle. The growing crowd of folk cheered for joy as Jock tottered backwards and forwards, eventually spilling the entire load. A chorus of voices chanted, 'Fine him his dues!' Agnes held up her hand for silence and, with jovial curses, Jock threw some coins from his pocket into a tin can, which Tam Wylie, the local blacksmith, thrust towards him.

'And any other of you who wants to pay your contribution to the drinks and ale purse, throw your coppers in here.' Tam flourished the can before the smiling faces of the tight-packed crowd that filled the hallway and doors of Jock and Agnes's farmhouse.

While bottles and mugs clinked and beverages were opened and consumed, the cake making began.

Agnes sprinkled dried herbs on the fire and spoke a prayer quietly to the bakers, and then the rhythmical tapping of baking boards began. Young Katharine rolled a piece of cake batter and slapped it skilfully on to her board. While they worked, the women sang a song of strong health, good luck, good neighbours and good cheer. During the song, Katharine was named the 'Toddler' and Lizzie, sitting next to her, was called the 'Hodler'. Katharine now threw her well-kneaded dough on to Lizzie's board. The pace of beating and dough-stretching was fast, and a steady rhythm kept up by slapping and tapping on the boards. The cake dough was passed around each of the women, in turn, around the circle. They skilfully shaped and stretched the mixture into an ever smoother and thinner pastry. Agnes named each of her baking maids in turn, 'Best Maid', 'Cheekiest Maid', 'Bonniest Maid', 'Worst Maid!' and 'Kindliest Maid'. Each name was met with a loud roar of approval and laughter from the onlookers. By the time the mixture reached Agnes, it was as round as the moon and smooth as a looking glass, stretched to paper-thin perfection. The women all bowed reverently to Agnes and sang a line about the Queen of the Cake and the Queen of the Fair looking out for all lost souls and weary travellers.

Agnes was blessed and named 'The Toaster'. She set the fine disc of sweet dough on to the griddle and placed it on the fire. As she cooked the first of the cakes, she proclaimed that it was to 'Be given to Major Brown to relieve his tedium, now that his dear wife had departed for the West Indies!' The crowd roared with laughter at the in-joke of the time, about a well-known pompous cuckold, while Jock ran back across the white circle to put more wood on the fire. The chant 'Fine him his dues!' to pay for more ale and whisky grew ever louder and all the money left in Jock's pockets was emptied into the drinks kitty.

Then, more balls of sweetened oat dough were patted and shaped, thrown and passed around the women at lightning speed. The song they sang helped their hands to dance out the perfect pastries. As the last dollop of batter was sent around, from east to west, by the skilful priestesses of baking, something quite spectacular happened: the pastry was so delicate and fine that as it was thrown from the last board towards the Toaster, the wafer-thin cake, caught by the warm updraft of the fire, floated past Agnes's griddle pan and disappeared up the chimney.

The women banged their elm boards down triumphantly and a cheer of ecstasy filled the house and out into the surrounding fields and lanes.

The ceremony was concluded with the cakes being wrapped in waxed paper. They would be taken to the Fair the following week and given freely to visitors and strangers, as a gesture of hospitality, which would hopefully bring the town and its people good luck for the coming year. Jock got down on his knees and hastily rubbed away the white circle so that the party could flow into the kitchen. Each baker was given a drop of their favourite tipple and the fiddler began a tune for the guests to begin dancing.

Curious children pushed forward to ask Agnes what had happened to the cake that had disappeared up the chimney?

Agnes laughed with delight, as she held court, sitting next to the fire. 'Well, you bairns gather round and I'll tell ye the story of the wee bannock that flew away up the chimney.

'That wee bannock was no for going to St Luke's Fair and being eaten by a stranger, so instead it flew away up high and then ran away doon tae Rutherglen Village. There it spied the church manse and away into the hoose it flew. Well, the minister and his wife were having tea and they liked the look o that sweet bannock, so they chased it aboot the parlour and she threw her knitting at it and he threw his sermon at it, but the bannock was fast and flew right off doon the road and intae the farmer's field. Well, the plough horses saw that wee bannock and they thought it would make a very tasty treat and so they chased the cake aboot the field, but it was no for being eaten by a horse either, and it flew right over the hedge and doon the street to the Blacksmith's Forge. Well, you know ole Tam the blacksmith, he's always hungry, and he saw that bannock and thought it would be good with some cheese and ale, but oh no that wee cake wasn'y happy with that either and off it flew towards the Kirk.

'Well, all the craws on the Kirk spire spotted the tasty wee bannock coming their way and they started tae squabble aboot which one o them was going to have the bannock for its supper. So the bannock flew right doon into a hole beneath the church wall. It thought it would be safe there, away from the hungry corbies, but guess who lived doon the hole in the kirk-yard? Tod the fox, of course! And when he smelled oor fine wee soul-cake, why, he gobbled that bannock all up, so we'll never see that cake ever agin!

'An that's the story of the runaway bannock for ye!'

25

SAINT KENTIGERN, THE PATRON SAINT OF GLASGOW

Saint Kentigern, better known as Saint Mungo, is the Patron Saint of Glasgow. He was said to have been born in 518 CE at Culross, on the north side of the Firth of Forth. His mother was Taneu (or Thenew), daughter of Leudonus, the half-pagan King of Leudonia (Lothian) better known as Lot, King of the Northern Gododdin. He wanted his daughter to marry Ewan, the son of Erwegende, a high lord of Strathclyde. This would help strengthen the pagan kings of Scotland's kingdoms against the threat of invasion from the Angles who were living in the south of Scotland and growing ever stronger. Taneu, however, was a recent convert to Christianity and refused to have any kind of relationship with Ewan. Lot threatened to send her to live with swineherds, 'in perpetual prostitution' (Aberdeen Breviary, p.66) if she would not form an allegiance with Ewan. Taneu still would not agree to the match with the Briton lord, and so her father sent her to the swineherds' hut. Fortunately for the young princess, one of the swineherds was also a convert to Christianity and he protected her. He did not, however, manage to prevent Ewan, who just happened to be dressed in women's clothes, from finding Taneu and raping her in the pig-keepers' hut!

In Jocelyn of Furness's hagiography of Mungo, written in about 1185, he continues this story with the pagan father having his now pregnant daughter thrown from a hillside (Traprain Law) in a cart as a heathen and barbaric punishment for being pregnant before marriage. This was meant to finish her off, but in this tale, she is unharmed by the fall, miraculously saved by the hand of God. She is then set adrift in a coracle on the Firth of Forth, where she washes up 25 miles away in Culross. Here, St Serf takes her in to his religious house, where young monks are trained, and Tenau gives birth to a son, Mungo.

As pagan beliefs were more inclined to accept, if not expect, pregnancy before marriage, and there is no evidence of anyone being killed by the Britons in this way, let alone an important king's daughter, and the child really was Ewan's, it is more likely that the stubborn and zealously Christian pregnant princess was sent to St Serf by her father to make sure the child was safe and Tenau kept out of the way of the pagan household.

In Culross, Teanu's child was named Kentigern, meaning 'high lord', but he was better known by his other name of Mungo, which means 'dear one'. Many legends exist about Mungo growing up here. The most well-known are the stories that explain the insignia on the Glasgow Coat of Arms. There is a rhyme to accompany the symbols of a tree with a bird in it, a fish with a ring in its mouth, and a bell:

> *There's the tree that never grew,*
> *There's the bird that never flew,*
> *There's the fish that never swam,*
> *There's the bell that never rang.*

The tree and the bird refer to a hazel twig and a robin, two stories from Mungo's stay in Culross. The twig is said to have burst into flames in Mungo's hands when he desperately needed to light a fire that, under his watch, had gone out. The robin was Serf's pet that

Mungo miraculously brought back to life after other boys at the abbey had killed it in an attempt to get Mungo into trouble. (The thirteenth-century Sprouston Breviary *states that it was Mungo who pulled the head off the robin in a rage, but he then prayed for God to restore the creature back to life, for fear of what Serf will do to him when he finds out!)*

The fish with a ring in its mouth is a story concerning Glasgow, or perhaps Cadzow, another Lanarkshire location, and will be told in full later within this chapter.

The bell was said to be gifted to Mungo by the Pope on one of his trips to Rome.

26

HOW MUNGO CAME TO GLASGOW

Mungo left Culross at about the age of twenty-three. He didn't go by choice, but rather with all of his fellow students chasing after him. They hated him so much that he had to flee for his life with St Serf by his side for protection. They didn't have time to wait for a ferry, or for good weather to cross the water. Mungo escaped by way of another miracle. Jocelyn of Furness wrote in *The Life of Saint Kentigern*:

The crossing was made over a little arm of the sea by means of a bridge, which is called by the inhabitants the Pons Serani, and Mungo looked back to the bank and saw the waters, which earlier had stood in a heap, flowing back with force and filing the channel of Mallena – even overflowing the above-mentioned bridge and totally denying passage to anyone trying to cross the river.

Parting the waters for Mungo's escape from Culross was just the start of a very long night for the young disciple. Poor old Serf stood on the opposite bank of the river crying out to Mungo not to leave him, but Mungo had no option, his fellow initiates were after his blood. Serf, who was now a very old man, returned to Culross and died shortly afterwards.

Mungo carried on, as instructed by Serf, to the house of Fergus at Kearnach, by St Ninian's Church, near Stirling. Fergus was very ill and close to death when young Mungo arrived, but Fergus had been given a vision from the Lord and was waiting for Mungo. He told him what he was to do with his body, after death, and then the old man promptly died.

The next morning, Mungo took Fergus's body out of the house, where a specially made cart was waiting, ready for the holy man's corpse. There was no horse or mule to pull the funeral load. Mungo followed the instructions given by Fergus on his sickbed the night before and went out into the fields, where two wild bulls came stampeding towards Mungo. He raised his hands calmly and the animals slid to a stop in front of him. He turned, calling on them, and they followed him meekly to the cart. Here they were harnessed on to the shafts of the cart, while Mungo climbed up on to the seat. He then commanded the wild beasts to pull them towards the place God had ordained, and the bulls obeyed. Followed by a great gathering of people, the funeral procession made its way to Cathures, later known as Glasgu (now Glasgow). The bulls came to a halt near some ancient trees in a peaceful glade beneath a wooded hill. Along one side ran a beautiful burn with cool, fresh water. The wild bulls began to graze on the sweet meadow grass and wild herbs growing all about. Mungo and the many pilgrims who had walked along with the cart from Stirling, and those who had joined the procession along the way, stopped to rest under the shade of the trees.

There was already a small group of Christians living in Glasgow, led by two monks: Telleyr and Anguen. When they heard that a great funeral party had arrived that day, they came to greet them. They were amazed at the throng of worshippers gathered in the glade. They explained to Mungo – or Kentigern, as people were now calling him – that the location the bulls had led them to was a special place for the people of the old religion. The hill above them was a sacred Druid grove and had been for many centuries. Also, the meadow by the burn where they were standing had been consecrated by St Ninian, who had brought Christianity to Scotland in much earlier times. Kentigern rejoiced at this news and declared to the crowd that this was where they must bury Fergus. Telleyr protested, telling Kentigern and his followers that no one could be buried here. Most of the inhabitants of Glasgu and surrounding lands were not yet converted to Christianity. If the Christians desecrated a sacred site of the Druids, there would be terrible consequences. Kentigern laughed at this and preached a sermon for all to hear about the word of God being sacred above all. The multitude of followers knelt and prayed and praised Kentigern. Anguen rejoiced at Kentigern's holy words and fell to his knees in veneration of this great man of God. Telleyr watched in horror as the crowd dug a grave and buried Fergus. This was such an important place to the worshippers of the old Celtic ways that he knew there would be trouble.

Kentigern did not mind one little bit that this was a pagan place of worship. His mission was to destroy the old unholy practices and bring the ignorant people to his God. He went to live with Telleyr and Anguen. While Anguen was in complete awe of Kentigern and happy to follow his preaching, Telleyr had been living peacefully with the Celts and pagan rulers. He practised and enjoyed a tolerant and accepting way to live side by side with them; his Christianity was compatible with many of their ancient nature-based beliefs and so acceptance was his motto. Kentigern's approach was entirely the opposite of Telleyr's, Kentigern refused to tolerate this type of Celtic Christianity. As far as he was concerned, anyone who did not live and worship as he did should not be allowed to live. Kentigern had declared war on the old pagan religion and their Druids, many of whom tried to reclaim their sacred land near the Druid hill and Molendinar Burn. In the following months, anyone who tried to remove Fergus's grave, or conduct nature worship on this ancient site, had a mysterious accident and died. Death never seemed to be far away for folk who challenged Kentigern, including Tellyr's own sudden end. Not long after Kentigern's arrival in Glasgow, while carrying the heavy limb of a tree, Telleyr supposedly tripped on a rock and was crushed to death by the tree.

27

THE BATTLE BETWEEN MORKEN AND KENTIGERN

Established in his new parish, Kentigern worked diligently to increase his followers and so spread the word of God. He lived with Brother Anguen by the banks of the Molendinar and farmed nine acres of rich arable land. When he needed to plough the land and no cattle were available, he tamed the wild deer from the woods to pull his plough iron. Once, he even ploughed with a wild wolf. This creature had killed and eaten one of the stags, so Kentigern used the scriptures to subdue its wild nature and lead it to the yoke, where it was duly set to work, pulling the plough beside the other deer. The Celtic pagans of Strathclyde were often known as the Stags, the deer being their sacred animal emblem, so perhaps it was really they whom Kentigern yoked to his plough.

One year, however, the harvest failed badly and Kentigern and the monks by the Molendinar were left with no food provisions. Kentigern was forced to go to the local High Chief, Morken, Lord of Strathclyde, and beg for help. Morken had not converted to Christianity. His chief advisor was Cathen, a head Druid, highly respected amongst the people of the old religion. They had no reason to like Kentigern and many reasons to hate him. Since Kentigern had arrived in Glasgow he had steadily increased his authority. As mentioned, whenever anyone protested against Kentigern defiling the sacred ancestral lands of the Celts of Strathclyde, they seemed to have mysterious accidents and die. The King of Strathclyde, Tutugal, had converted to Christianity and the doctrine that Kentigern preached complemented a less egalitarian society, which suited the King well. He was happy to encourage Kentigern's enterprises in Glasgow, so Morken, who was subject to the King, had to be careful around Bishop Kentigern.

Kentigern pleaded with Morken to share some of his harvested grain with him and his starving religious community. However, Morken mocked the bishop.

'Cast thy care upon the Lord, and he will sustain thee.'

The pagan chief delighted in telling the Christians how lame he thought their god was. 'I, however, who seek neither the Kingdom of God nor his justice, am increased with all prosperity and an abundance of all things smile on me … your faith is empty, and your preaching is false.'

Kentigern did not give up asking for help and so, according to Jocelyn's *Life of Kentigern*, Morken laid down a spiritual challenge to him.

'If, trusting in your God and without human hands you are able to transfer to your dwelling all my coarse meal which is held in my storehouse that you see, I concede and give to you freely from my spirit and I will submit faithfully to your petitions concerning other things.'

The Christians left Morken's Hall, and Kentigern had to do some serious praying, or perhaps some serious grain store raiding! Jocelyn's text tells us that after Mungo had prayed for God to intervene, a mammoth storm rose up and caused the waters of the River Clyde to rise in a huge wave. This tsunami broke over the banks of the river at Partick, where Morken's barns were situated. This great deluge circled around the grain stores, lifting them up onto a gigantic wave, which swept all the way upstream along the Molendinar Burn, and deposited them at Kentigern's church. Miraculously, none of the contents of the barns had been soaked or spoiled by the great deluge.

Needless to say, this did not go down well with the pagan chief and the Druids. Morken was ready to attack Kentigern and his band of fanatical, grain-stealing followers, so King Tutugal intervened and set up a meeting between them. At this meeting, Kentigern remained pious and denied any wrong-doing, which angered Morken even more. Eventually, the non-Christians snapped. Cathen, Head Druid, cursed the arrogance and lies of the Christians, while Morken resorted to violence against Kentigern, flinging him down to the ground and having a swift kick at the Christian zealot.

Tutugal was mortified; things had gone too far and all parties were sent their separate ways to cool down. Jocelyn's account suggests that the wicked Druid Cathen fell from his horse and died of a broken neck as he left the fateful meeting and that Morken died from tumours in the foot with which he had kicked Kentigern very soon after. The majority of people living in Glasgow were followers of the old religion, who had been peacefully living alongside the Telleyr Christians without problems for a long time. This was changing and an ever-growing feeling of anger and unrest was developing in Glasgow, the Dear Green Place. Fearing a religious war, Tutugal and Kentigern decided that it may be best if the bishop left Glasgow before he too was murdered. Kentigern fled to Wales to live under the protection of Saint David.

28

THE FISH
AND THE RING

After Morken's death in Glasgow and King Tutugal's death, a new king took over Strathclyde, Rhydderch Hael, second son of Tutugal. He was a Christian convert, but his wife, Queen Languoreth, daughter of Morken, was not. Languoreth and her twin brother, Lailoken, were brought up in the old religion. Lailoken was in fact highly advanced in Druidry (the murdered Druid, Cathan, having been one of his teachers). Lailoken is known as the 'Wild Merlin' of the Lowland tradition. King Rhydderch invited Kentigern back to Glasgow. He needed a strong church leader and no one had yet come up to Bishop Kentigern's fervent Christian standards. Kentigern returned promptly. Even though he had started a church in Wales, he had tried St David's patience, and a change of residence now seemed like his best option. Once back in Glasgow, he could continue his quest to end the religion of the old pagan ways.

It was at about this time, with Kentigern back and Lailoken returned from his own exile in the forest (Lailoken became mentally unwell after the Battle of Arderydd against the Angles, and lived wild, in southern Scotland for many years), that Queen Languoreth got herself into a lot of bother with the King. Born and brought up at Cadzow Castle, high above the Avon Gorge, eleven miles south of Glasgow, Languoreth was known as the Queen of Cadzow. Now she was married to Rhydderch, most of their time was spent living at their palace in Partick, but they often came south to Cadzow to hunt in the abundant forests that surrounded the district. It was here, on their royal weekend hunting parties, where Languoreth fell disastrously in love with the young Laird o' Lee. One of the King's elite soldiers, Lee was many years younger than Languoreth's husband and also very attractive. As there had been peace in the Kingdom of Strathclyde since the Angles had been defeated at the Battle of Arderydd, the King and the Queen had enjoyed much pleasure time at their Lanarkshire hunting lodge. This had given the Queen many weeks in the company of the fit young soldier and finally she had given in to desire and they had become lovers.

No one was ever really sure if Rhydderch knew about his wife's lover. He was twelve years older than her, and although he was trying to embrace the ways of this new Christianity, he knew that Languoreth felt strongly about the Druids' right to teach and practise their vast knowledge of botany, astronomy and spirituality. He loved her very much and didn't want to force her to accept Kentigern's religion, especially with her twin brother, Lailoken, being such a wise man of the old faith. Whether he was turning a blind eye to his wife's affair or not, the day finally came when he was given no other option but to confront her. One of his men at court in Glasgow threatened to make a scandal out of the situation if it was allowed to continue. The office bearer had noticed that the Laird o' Lee was wearing Languoreth's ring and he implored the King to confront his wife and put an end to the adultery before the Monarch became a laughing stock throughout the realm. The Christian faction in his kingdom had been making their disapproval of his tolerance ever louder, and a reluctant Rhydderch knew he must now act to end his wife's affair.

During the next good spell of weather, the King took his best hunters and Queen out to Cadzow for exercise and sport. After a successful morning hunting, a wild boar was caught and roasted over a fire by the river. The men ate and drank, then stretched out for a nap in the sun. He encouraged them all to get a good sleep now, on the banks of the river, before returning to the castle for a night of feasting and dancing. Each man drank to that and rolled over to snooze under the willows, which hung down into the flowing waters of the Clyde. When Rhydderch was sure the young laird was asleep, he carefully prised the ring from his little finger. For a moment, as he looked at the wee golden ring and precious stone, he was overcome with sadness. This ring had been made especially for her, with gold from Leadhills and an expensive gem bought from traders. He had given it to her on their wedding day. Ryhdderch wasted no more time on sentimental thoughts and threw the ring into the waters of the Clyde. For a moment he felt like punching the bonny face of the laird as he slept, but the King controlled himself and gathered his dignity. He would enjoy the proper process of accusation and punishment far more than a fleeting angry outburst.

Accusation and punishment for Languoreth followed very quickly. Back at their lodgings, he asked her for the special ring that he had given her at their betrothal. Red-faced, Languoreth knew she was caught, but she made excuses and went to her chamber to fetch the ring for him. While away, she sent word to her lover to bring the ring to her immediately. The laird, of course, could not find it and returned his message via a serving man. The laird then made his escape and left his lover Queen to face the wrath of the King alone. Rhydderch went through the motions of making a public display of his anger and contempt for his Queen's infidelity before the informant and counsel. He admonished the Queen for her behaviour, threatened her with cruel punishment followed by death after three days, and sent her to be imprisoned in her own chamber. When he was left alone, the King felt sickened by the whole charade and despairingly sad. He still loved her very much.

Languoreth acted quickly, calling for her brother to help. Lailoken knew that the Christians wanted her punished for her adultery, but also because she was a pagan queen and not a convert to their scriptures. He advised her to bring Kentigern down to the castle to absolve her of her sin and in return she must offer herself as a Christian convert. This she did, and Kentigern was amazed and delighted at this change of character and heart in the Queen. Although he despised anything to do with sex, within or without marriage, he was willing to forgive such an important pagan and use her conversion to God as a weapon for good against the heathens of the land. Lailoken suggested that he come to the river and look for the ring with him, for he knew that this was where the King had thrown it.

Lailoken, accompanied by Kentigern, went to the spot where the hunting party had roasted their meat the day before and Lailoken threw a hook and line into the swell of the Clyde. He encouraged Kentigern to pray for his God's help, and as the bishop said a prayer, the Druid pulled out a fish, a big salmon. He gutted the fish and there inside its belly he found Languoreth's ring. Kentigern visited her in her chamber to give her absolution and begin her conversion to his religion.

As she agreed, knelt and began her prayer to the unseen, all-powerful God of all, Kentigern placed the ring in her lap. The lord had won a new soul for the Christian cause and Languoreth had won her life and freedom back.

King Rhydderch was overjoyed when she presented him with the ring. He took this as a sign of her innocence and made public her reprieve. Kentigern was extremely pleased with his own victory and made the most of it in the years to come. Languoreth never spoke of the true nature of the affair ever again during Rhydderch's life and they lived many long happy years together, but when he died, she shared the story far and wide.

29

THE WITCHES
OF POLLOK

*This tale from Glasgow comes from a time when witchcraft was
believed in by all levels of society, from kings and queens to illit-
erate peasants and everybody in-between. Witch hunting and
prosecuting was, however, an activity that belonged to the ruling
class. Sir George Maxwell, a member of the Scottish ruling elite,
owned the Pollok estate, a vast area of land with a castle in the
parish of Eastwood, in south Glasgow. (Pollok Castle was replaced
by Pollok House, a magnificent Georgian mansion, in the eighteenth century, which is situated in Pollok Park – where the Burrell
Collection is housed – and is open to the public.) Across the White
Cart Water from the castle was the small village of Polloktoun, long
since gone. Sir George was from a prominent Presbyterian family
and had been an active Covenanter during the years of religious
conflict. His affiliation to the Protestant Church and his extremist
views of rooting out evil and destroying witchcraft led Sir George to
be appointed to two commissions that prosecuted and executed so-
called witches, at Inverkip in 1662 and four years later in Gourock.*

*In 1676, Sir George believed himself to be the victim of witch-
craft, which led to the trial of six people (five of them executed) in
Paisley in 1677. This story was well documented through a letter*

that Sir George wrote outlining his experience to George Sinclair,
Professor of Philosophy at Glasgow College, and from his son John's
detailed account of his father's bewitching. This sensational true
tale gives us a very clear sense of people's witch beliefs in the latter
half of seventeenth-century Scotland.

Sir George Maxwell of Pollok (knighted by King Charles II) was
one of the most eminent men in the whole of Scotland. On 14
October 1676, he went to Glasgow on business to inspect his
soap and candle works, in Candleriggs. Soon after he arrived,
Sir George became ill. He collapsed in terrible pain, clutching
his chest and side. He was carried back home to Pollok Castle
and doctors were called. Sweat poured from the sick man, as he
groaned in agony, telling the doctors that it felt as though he
was being stabbed repeatedly in the right side.

Suspicion was already creeping into everyone's minds that
this could be the result of evildoing. Were Sir Maxwell's ail-
ments the result of malevolent practice? Could witches be
responsible for his sudden ill health? Sir George was, after all, a
man of high social standing with strict Presbyterian convictions,
and a keen prosecutor of witches. Earlier that same year he had
convicted witches and sentenced them to be put to death, down
the Clyde coast in Gourock. Sir George did not respond to any
medical treatments, and showed no signs of improving, leaving
the doctors baffled. Rumours of witchcraft grew louder.

A vagrant girl from the Highlands had arrived in Polloktoun
the previous month and become friends with Sir Maxwell's two
daughters. Anne and Marie Maxwell found the teenager to be
a fascinating creature, a breath of fresh air. Because the girl was
deaf and mute, they communicated with her through hand
gestures, drawing pictures and miming out their conversations.
The sisters had worked out that her name was Janet and she
was thirteen or fourteen years old. They enjoyed her company
immensely, as it all seemed like a fun game of charades. This

mute stranger also seemed to possess some mystical qualities of second sight and knowing the future. At least that's what the siblings hoped was true, as it was common belief at that time that deaf and mute people were gifted with psychic powers. One day, while Sir George was still lying in his bed, sick with this unknown illness, Janet pointed out a woman in a crowd at Polloktoun to the Maxwell girls and using gestures conveyed that this woman was responsible for Sir Maxwell's ill health. At first, they couldn't understand what their friend was trying to tell them, so Janet took them home. She went to one of the gentlewomen's closets, took some beeswax, plied it near the fire and moulded it into a little human figure. Pushing pins into the wax figurine, Janet showed the girls that their father was being hurt through an effigy, like this, and witchcraft.

Sir Maxwell's terrified daughters sent two of their father's servants, with Janet, to the house of the woman she said had made the wax figure that was causing his illness. Janet led them to the miller's widow, Jonet Maithie. The young girl marched right into the startled woman's home and pulled a little wax figurine from out of the chimney breast. As she handed it to Sir George's men, they gasped as they saw the three pins sticking out of the poppet. The widow was questioned as to the meaning of the wax doll but denied all knowledge of it, replying that it was the dumb girl's doing, and nothing to do with her. Young Janet managed to explain with gestures that Maithie's son had been caught stealing from Sir Maxwell's orchard and had been punished by Sir George. The mother was a disciple of the Devil and had made the image to harm Sir George. She wanted revenge for Maxwell banishing her boy from his estate, and forcing him to move some distance away to Darnley. The authorities were informed, and Jonet Maithie was imprisoned in Paisley so that a search for insensible marks on her body could be conducted. If any were found this, the people believed, would prove that she was in partnership with the Devil. Numerous insensible marks (moles and freckles) were found on Mrs Maithie, so she stayed in prison. The pins in the wax effigy – one in the chest and the deepest two in the right side – were removed, and the two serving men reported that the laird began to recover that same night. This blatant sensational-ism created much local gossip, the fuel on which the witch-hunts relied. Maxwell's son said of his father's illness, after the pins were removed, 'There was some abatement of Sir George's sickness, but not to any observable degree.'

Even with Jonet Maithie in prison, people still thought her evil influence was causing harm in Polloktoun. The Earl of Dundonald, who had granted Maithie's arrest warrant, was travelling in a party to his granddaughter's wedding at Eglington. As they passed the cottage of one of Jonet's daughters, the coach horses stopped in the road and refused to go past the house. After much persuasion, the men gave up and the riders in the party hitched their own horses to the coach. These horses too would not go past the cottage, turning their heads in the opposite direc-tion and fighting to get away from the place. In the end they had no choice but to abandon all plans of going to the wedding, turn around and go home.

Sir George started to get well around Christmas time that year, but then relapsed into illness in January 1677. Janet appeared to have been away from Polloktoun for a few days, but then she sent word to the Maxwell family that John Stewart, Jonet's son, had been carrying out his mother's work for Satan. He had made a clay effigy and roasted it before the fire with pins. It was now hidden beneath the bolster among the bedstraw. With Janet's remarkably detailed description, the authorities had no problem finding the clay figure and John Stewart and his young sister, Annabil, were arrested. They confessed to attending witch meet-ings and named three other local women who had been present at the effigy making, along with the Devil. All of them were arrested and put in Paisley Tolbooth, except for the Devil, who always seemed to evade capture!

During interrogation and at their trials the most incredible details of satanic practice emerged. Each of the accused seemed to have some resentment against Sir Maxwell, having suffered minor slights over the years from their landlord. Three of the women, Jonet Maithie, Bessie Weir and Marjory Craig, refused to admit any guilt or wrongdoing, but John and Annabil Maithie, and Margaret Jackson, who was eighty years old, confessed readily. The terms of the commission specified that no torture was to be used, however, Jonet Maithie was put in stocks in her cell after an effigy was found under her bed and one can only wonder at the conditions of the prison and the treatment from interrogators.

Fourteen-year-old Annabil gave vivid descriptions of her dealings with the Devil, describing him as, 'A man with black clothes, a blue band, and white handcuffs [Shirt cuffs].' He also wore hoggers (footless stockings) over his cloven feet. At the witch meetings, the Devil had helped in the making of the effigies. These effigies were passed around from hand to hand, with each person stating their name and saying, 'I have the portraiture of Sir George Maxwell of Nether Pollok in my hand and I consent unto his death.' John Stewart confessed that his mother had given himself and his sister to the Devil when they were still in her womb, but that when they came of age they had to give themselves to him again in a satanic ritual. Annabil described that 'she put her hand to the crown of her head, and the other to the sole of her foot, and did give herself up to the Devil'. This was a commonly reported ritual all over Scotland, offering everything in-between the two hands to Satan. In return Annabil was offered a new coat. At the end of the ritual the Devil lay with her, and she found his manhood to be 'cold as ice'.

The three confessions were enough to sentence all six of the accused to death, but Annabil was sent to prison on account of her 'nonage' (youth). They were hanged at Gallowgreen, Paisley, on 20 February 1677. A raven flew towards the gallows

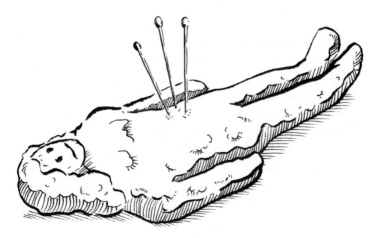

as Bessie was hanged and the hangman and onlookers gasped in fear at this portent of evil. The effigies that had led to this sad scene of execution were wrapped in cloth, smashed and thrown on to the bonfire, which consumed the five corpses. Sir George himself, 'worn to a shadow', died of a 'sweating sickness' in April that same year. Janet Douglas, the young girl from the Highlands, recovered from the swelling of her throat and tongue by taking a cure, Album Graecum (dog poo, turned white, then powdered and mixed with honey). After she regained her ability to speak, she claimed never to have been mute at all.

She used her psychic visions to detect more effigies and witches. While moving from town to town, she became a celebrity and many more people died after her accusations led to arrests and witchcraft trials. Eventually, she was imprisoned in Edinburgh, accused of 'inciting the crowd'. By this time, hundreds of people were flocking to see and hear her. Many eminent scholars came to interview her and some believed strongly that she did have true psychic ability, while others thought that she was a charlatan. Janet was finally whipped and sentenced to deportation, although no sea captains were willing to take a woman with her reputation on board their ships. There is no record of Janet Douglas leaving the country, but some suggested that she was the illegitimate child of a noble person and that he helped her to disappear into the safety of anonymity. We may never know what truly happened to this unusual Scottish witch-accuser of the seventeenth century.

30

THE SHEEP'S HEID

Govan is one of the oldest settlements along the River Clyde. Here you can visit an exceptional collection of early medieval carved stones, housed inside Govan Parish Church. These thirty-one monumental stones date back to sometime between the ninth and eleventh centuries. Govan appears to have been an important place at the heart of the Britonnic (British) Kingdom of Strathclyde, linked to the Royal Palaces at Partick by a ford across the River Clyde. A sixth-century (565 CE) monastery is believed to have been founded here by Constantine, a contemporary of Columba and Kentigern. The remains of a small hill, called a Doomster Hill, were also discovered near to the church in Govan. These hills were where judgements and laws were made, so a type of early parliament.

The Britons of Strathclyde were quashed by the Scots of the Gaelic Kingdom of Dalriada, who took over Govan as their own religious centre – they brought their own saint, Constantine, although there is much debate about which Constantine was which and there are another three King Constantines connected to the area to confuse things further. A beautifully carved stone sarcophagus dedicated to Constantine is part of the remarkable Govan stones collection. By the eleventh century, Govan must have been a cult religious centre as Christianised Danish settlers and the Anglians of Northumberland buried their high-status dead here. Five Viking Hogback burial stones are also displayed in the parish church. David I established a new diocese in Glasgow in the early twelfth century and revived the cult of St Kentigern, thus leading to a decline in St Constantine's importance.

Govan, however, continued to flourish, primarily in fishing and farming, but coal mining and new trades and crafts were established as the centuries unfolded.

The Govan Weavers Society was formed in 1756 as a guild of master weavers. They held an annual parade on the first Friday of June, known as Govan Fair Day – which continues to this day. The society's banner bears a ram's head.

The story of this sheep's heid (head) was believed to have originated in the fifteenth century, when the village of Govan was productive with hand-loom weaving, silk-making, potteries, salmon fishing and agriculture.

James Burnett came from the arable communities north of Glasgow; a country lad looking for work. He was broad-framed, with an honest face and a canny twinkle in his eye. In church on Sundays, many of the village girls liked to glance in his direction and if he looked back, their hearts would race and their cheeks blush red. However, the lass that caught Jamie's eye and made his heart skip a beat was Tessa Brown. Tessa was the minister's scullery maid; nineteen years old, glowing with health and youth. Shiny flaxen tresses of hair sprang out from under her bonnet and her eyes gleamed amber and innocent. Not only was she pretty, but several years of hard work lighting fires, carrying buckets and scrubbing the floors of Minister Caldwell's large church manse had made her lithe and strong.

As the months rolled by and the seasons changed, young James focused his attentions on Tessa. The mutual attraction between them developed into a firm friendship. When they met, two hearts beat faster and their desire for each other grew stronger. The young couple were falling deeply in love. They managed to meet two or three times a week, but they both longed to be together every day.

On Whitsun Sunday, after a very long church service, as the congregation were leaving the church, James finally got a moment alone with Tessa. At the back of the chapel he held her hand, gazed lovingly into her eyes and asked his sweetheart to be his wife. She was overjoyed and said, without hesitation, 'Yes.' Now, all that remained was for James to ask Minister Caldwell for his permission.

However, that evening when he went to the manse to ask the minister for his blessings and consent to marry Tessa, he was met with a cold and bitter response. Caldwell had been well aware of the couple's growing fondness for each other, and he made it clear that he did not approve of their relationship. He tried to mask his dislike of James, whom he considered to be nothing more than a common farm labourer, with a false concern for Tessa's long-term welfare. He forbade James from spending any further time with his maid, saying that his need for her services was far greater than a mere farm boy's. Caldwell asserted that Tessa must remain at the manse where she was not only serving himself, the minister, but ultimately she was serving God. James was sent packing, threatened with being sacked from his work on the neighbouring farm if he dared to bother the minister or Tessa again.

Now, as you can imagine, neither Tessa nor James was happy about this turn of events. On his way back home to the farm bunkhouse, James stopped off at the local inn to console himself with company and a drink. As he sat at the bar with his mug of ale, the local men listened to James' tale of woe and thwarted love. Soon enough, everyone in the place had an opinion about Minister Caldwell and his harsh judgement of the young couple. After one or two more pints, the local worthies schemed a way to secure James' and Tessa's future together.

The next evening, James climbed over the manse wall and slipped undetected into the herb garden, where he met and spoke with his darling Tess. An escape plan was agreed between

them that would free her from a life of servitude to the bitter
minister and assure them a new life as a couple.

After the bells chimed midnight, James set off with his
backpack, which contained all his worldly possessions, and his
sheepdog Bessie, whom he had trained from when she was a
tiny puppy. He met with his trusted friend Charlie Hopkins
at the cross, and the two men and their dogs – Charlie had
brought his deerhound Willow – made their way stealthily to
the pasture land that surrounded the church and manse. Tessa
was waiting for her lover behind the graveyard wall – her bag
filled with her clothes, the candlestick her grandmother had
given her and her Bible.

As the clouds rolled over the moon, what was happening
in the field beside the church was barely visible. Bessie was
rounding up the minister's sheep and herding them swiftly
and quietly out of the open gate to where James, Charlie and
Tessa stood, waiting tensely. Tessa followed the flock along the
lane and out of the village. Several local men, who had been
at the inn with Jamie the
night before, were stra-
tegically positioned at
the entries of closes and
crossroads through-
out the village, each
helping to move the
sheep in the direction
of the road that led out
of Govan.

Charlie stayed with
Jamie, while Bessie was sent
into the field to skilfully separate out the best young ram from
what was left of the flock. Jamie
sent Bessie to herd this ram up the

road to join Tessa and the ewes, leaving just one old ram and two scraggy, lame ewes in the pasture. The old, startled ram bellowed so loudly during the sheep-rustling operation that Charlie had no choice but to send his dog into the field. Willow was a fine deer hunter; on command she swiftly brought the ram down. It was a quick and natural death, the old sheep's windpipe crushed by the bitch's powerful jaws in just a few seconds.

Jamie shook hands with his friend and accomplice, Charlie, and then sprinted off to catch up with his dear Tess and the minister's flock of sheep. News had spread like wildfire around the village about the evening's excitement, and those folk who were not sound asleep in their beds came out into the night to say goodbye and give the eloping couple their blessings.

Tessa, Jamie, Bessie and a flock of God's own sheep left Govan that evening for a new life somewhere in the hills and glens of Scotland.

The Govan villagers soon settled back to sleep on that most unusual of evenings, dreaming of jumping sheep and love's young promise. Minister Caldwell awoke bright and early in the morning. As he rose from his bed and looked from the manse window, he was startled by the sight of his old ram's head, severed from its body, stuck on top of a bloody wooden stave. The pole with the sheep's head had been planted boldly in the middle of the empty pasture.

Without Tessa, the serving maid, to cook his dinner that evening, Minister Caldwell reluctantly made his way to the local inn, where he sat sourly and ate the only dish on offer, mutton stew!

31

THE GOVAN CAT

For centuries merchant ships brought flax to supply the thriving weaving trade along the River Clyde. But around the year 1720 they also brought diseases and a new breed of rat. Govan, sitting snugly on the south bank of the Clyde with its newly deepened channel, boasted the best docking areas for the largest of the eighteenth-century commercial sailing ships. Great bales of flax filled the dark, wooden holds, and among this golden, dusty cargo came stowaways: the brown rat, originally from central Asia. It used to be believed that the fleas, living in the rats' fur, carried the plague, but now it is thought to have been a virus, similar to Ebola, transmitted through close contact, human to human. Nothing could stop the virus from spreading among the families who lived in the cramped and draughty weavers' and fishers' cottages. Children shared beds with many siblings and disease spread unchecked through crowded homes and busy streets. The first symptom was the glands in people's throats becoming so painfully swollen that swallowing was almost impossible. Then boils and pustules formed under the arms, around the ears, in the groin, on all of the body's glands. After four to five days of unbearable misery, death released the poor victim from their disease-racked body. The deadly plague advanced through families and neighbours, claiming thousands of lives in a matter of weeks.

In the centre of Govan stood the ancient village cross. Folk gathered here to trade goods, listen to news, buy cures from travelling doctors and barbers and share gossip. Hovels and houses, market barrows, blacksmith yards and hostelries formed two main roads, which led to the cross. This was the heart of Govan, where the community and commerce thrived. At the end of each working day, folk discarded their rubbish in the communal midden. This was situated on the edge of the town square where the refuse from the bustle of humanity and their associated trades in food, fowl, fish and quadrupeds was dumped to decay and rot. Hungry dogs, cats, birds and rats rooted about for leftover food, fish heads and guts among the decomposing piles of garbage and animal dung. At night they were joined by foxes and badgers; a cacophony of creatures could be heard howling and fighting over their right to hunt the rats and mice attracted here by the stench of the middens.

The big brown rats from the flax ships descended on the Govan rubbish dump and thrived. They were bigger than the black rats that had lived in Britain for many centuries. The resident black rats were vegetarians and liked to live in and around houses, but the fearsome, new rat species ate almost everything and didn't appear to be scared of anything; even the local Govan street dogs were frightened of them. With no predators tough enough to keep the rats down, they multiplied quickly in the mild, damp west coast climate. The fearsome brown rats now owned Govan Cross.

The good and the worthy townsfolk of Govan made valiant efforts to kill these unwelcome visitors. Notices were made in church on Sunday and the town crier declared that 'Prizes and Bold Sums of Gold' were to be given to the owner of any dogs brought to the cross for the purpose of 'Killing Rats'. Many fine lurchers, collies, terriers, and all manner of hunting dogs were brought to the town and set loose on the filthy kingdom of the super-rats. Few, if any, of the poor canines were a match for them. Many dogs fought to the death in their attempts to dispatch the rats, but all of them suffered and perished from rat bites, which later became infected. Desperate times descended on Govan as disease spread unchecked.

However, one day, a young fisher lass's luck changed when a merchant ship sailed into harbour and she spotted a tanned and wily sailor walking past her fish creel. He stopped for a moment, attracted by her smile, and inquired after the nearest ale house. Something in his dark piercing eyes and his swarthy, chiselled features made Mary pay him a little more friendly attention than she did to other sailors. Her smiles were returned by the seaman in equal measure and he persuaded her to accompany him to the bar that she recommended. As she led him up towards the cross and the inn of her choosing, he remarked on the foul smell of the middens. Mary told him the sad tale of the new breed of rats that had brought so much misery and pestilence to the small town.

While Mary and her merchant sailor dined on broth and bread, he told her about his ship's cat, and how it might just be the answer to the town's problem.

A further meeting was arranged between the two and later that night Mary's new love came to her lodging house carrying a fish creel that she had loaned to him earlier that day. Inside the wicker basket was the largest ginger tom cat that Mary or her sailor had ever seen. When they showed the cat to the landlady and other lodgers, they all remarked on the animal's incredible size and concluded that it must be the biggest cat in Scotland! The sailor and Mary carried the creature to the midden at the cross. Long before they reached the stinking piles of rubbish, the sound of scratching and the squeals of rats could be heard. The man put his hand into Ginger's carry case and rubbed affectionately around the cat's broad head and chin. The big cat purred so loudly that the woven willow basket vibrated.

'Right then, big Ginger lad,' the sailor spoke fondly to the animal, 'looks like you've got a job to do in this good town and I'll wager my year's pay that you'll rid this place of the filthy long-tails before my shore leave is up.'

He let Ginger out among the piles of rotting waste and the creature wasted no time, pouncing immediately on the first rat he saw. The sheer weight of the oversized moggie broke the rat's neck – the rat cull had begun.

Throughout his shore leave, Mary's new boyfriend stayed with her in her rooms near the cross. Word had spread quickly about his confident wager that his ship's cat would kill all of the troublesome rats. The odds were agreed and bets placed. By the end of the week the rat population was decimated and Ginger had become a hero. The town council agreed to pay for the cat's upkeep and Mary was made his official guardian. Rumour has it that her sailor won enough money on the wager to buy permanent leave from his ship. He married his Govan fisher lass and together they lived happily with their king of cats, Ginger. Eventually the couple moved

into the new flats built when Govan was once more a flourishing town. Many stories were told about the ginger tom-cat's
eventual demise. One tale described a fanciful battle between
Ginger and the King of the Rats; both cat and rat dying as a
result of their wounds. However, my favourite story described
how the ferocious tom never fully acclimatised to living on the
top floor of the tenement building and that in his old age he
jumped through the open window to pounce on the pigeons
who were cooing cheekily on the window ledge. The great
feline fell to the ground several storeys below. Although the
fall didn't kill him, he was never quite right in the head again.
After many attempts to catch the window-ledge pigeons, old
Ginger, the biggest, fiercest cat to ever grace the middens of
Govan, finally died.

Someone, possibly Mary, who was by then a wealthy widow,
left enough money in her will to have Ginger immortalised in a
fine sandstone carving, which still graces the wall of the Cardell
Hall building in Govan to this day.

32

THE VAMPIRE
WITH THE
IRON TEETH

This story from Glasgow is based on a real incident that has become enshrined in Scottish folklore, and is the most modern story from the Glasgow selection, taking place in September 1954. An Act of Parliament that banned the sale of comics that showed 'incidents of a repulsive or horrible nature' to children was passed in 1955. This was to protect them from the perceived harm that American horror comics could potentially do to their young, impressionable minds. A gang of children hunting a vampire with iron teeth in the Gorbals area of Glasgow was cited as the reason that this bill needed to be passed in Parliament.

There is a long tradition of children gathering en masse to hunt for various types of ghosts, vampires or monsters in Glasgow. In 1935–36 and 1938 hundreds of children were reported to have gone hunting for Spring-Heeled Jack in the Hutchestown–Gorbals area over several nights. This particular urban horror character first appeared in London in 1837 – he was a tall, thin devilish apparition with a tight white oilskin garment, cloak and horned mask. His eyes burned red while he breathed blue flames over his victims, tore their clothing with iron claws, and then sprang away over high walls and buildings to escape capture. Spring-Heeled Jack became a popular character in the Penny Dreadfuls – early horror magazines – and his cult spread all over Britain.

This type of story demonstrates very neatly how folklore is made and passed from one generation to the next.

Robbie and Tam were nearly seven, which is why they both felt they were old enough to skip up the High Street, one blustery autumn day, after school. Robbie's and Tam's parents would not have been happy if they knew that their wee boys were going a mile through Glasgow City, in the opposite direction from home. However, the boys thought that being so close to their seventh birthdays entitled them to a little more freedom than they were allowed as mere six-year-olds. Anyway, they were only going to the Necropolis, the big old graveyard on the hill behind the cathedral. It was conker season and Tam's big brother had told him that the largest trees and best conkers were up in the cemetery in the 'toun'.

Going up the High Street was another world to the boys; shops, tramcars, trucks and so many people, the bustle of the city centre was mesmerising to two wee lads from the Gorbals. It took them an age to finally make their way up the hill to the oldest part of Glasgow, next to the great monumental cathedral. They entered the Necropolis through an old stone archway, past the gatehouse and over the Bridge of Sighs. Robbie reminded Tam that the bridge was haunted by all the lost souls whose coffins had been carried over it on their way to burial in the cemetery, which the pair were now entering.

'An if you hear anyone cryin or sighin, you know a ghost who cannae rest in peace is after ye!' Robbie teased, then gave a long howl to frighten Tam.

Both of them raced, full of high spirits, and a hint of fear, laughing and moaning like ghosts, into the Necropolis. Tam glanced back behind him, just to make sure no spectres had followed them from the haunted bridge. Robbie led on along the path, which wound its way up and around the steep Hill of the Dead. The boys paused every now and then at a stone angel, or imposing obelisk, to read the inscriptions. Tam's reading was better than his friend's, but many of the words were too long and obscure for him to understand, so they satisfied themselves by repeating names and dates.

Robbie was first to spot the pair of old boots sticking out from inside a broken tomb. He stopped in horror, and signalled silently but frantically to Tam to be quiet and come and look.

Tam was instantly scared, but then decided his pal was probably just trying to frighten him again, and so he shouted at his friend, 'Oh aye, you seen anither ghost Rab? Has it got a heid under its arm?'

Robbie grabbed Tam by the arm and shoved his hand over his friend's mouth. He hissed quietly, 'Ssh't you dummy! Look, there in the big grave-hoose, a pair of legs an boots!'

The lads gawped at two worn-out old boots, attached to a pair of dirty and frayed men's trousers, which appeared to have legs in them. Neither boots or legs were moving. Both boys were at first convinced they were looking at a dead body, in its grave. Then Tam picked up the nearest stone he could find and hurled it at the boots. It missed and clanked noisily off of a broken tombstone. Rab earthed out a few pebbles from the neatly trimmed embankment and together the boys aimed their missiles, until one or two hit their mark, the mystery legs.

Old Jock, a gentleman of no fixed abode, woke up from his nap in the uncared-for tomb of some deceased bigwig from yesteryear. Something had hit his leg and then it happened again, he was under assault. The old tramp sat up fast and yelled out in pain, rubbing his sore shin. He saw the two children, with rocks in their hands, standing staring at him with wide eyes and astonished looks on their faces.

'Stop that ye wee buggers. Whit d'ye think yer doin, hurlin yuckies at me. Ah was just havin a wee nap!'

Tam and Robbie had seen plenty of old vagrants like Jock before, so that wasn't what was bothering them. They had never seen one like this though, or encountered any in a graveyard. This old man had black stumps for teeth. The boys stood frozen to the spot, staring at the man, with their mouths wide open.

Jock saw the look of terror on the laddies' faces. Realising how young the boys were, he stopped yelling at them and tried a more friendly approach, giving them a big smile. Tam and Robbie transfixed on the jagged row of grey and black teeth, as the man grimaced at them, and began backing away. Jock tried even harder to win their trust and began singing a bairn's song for them:

Wee Willie Winkie rin through the toon,
Upstairs an'doon stairs in his dressing goon.
Tirlin' at the window, crying at the lock,
Are the weans in their bed, for it's now ten o' clock.

Tam and Robbie looked at each other in confusion. Jock's attempt to win them over with the well-known nursery song was scaring them even more. This bedtime chant immediately reminded them of their grannies' favourite threat, at bedtime, when they were trying to get them to go to sleep.

'Jenny with the airn teeth will get you!'

'Jenny wi the airn teeth will come sink her teeth into your plump wee sides and take you to her den.'

Everyone's granny in Glasgow knew Alexander Anderson's scary poem, 'Jenny Wi the Airn Teeth', from their school days, and every child was terrified of the dreaded night when Jenny would sink her iron teeth into their flesh and 'take them to her den'.

The boys were edging further and further away, but the tramp was on his feet and ambling after them. He waved his arms about and then pointed towards a big granite memorial. He shouted out, 'Yon's William Miller's stone, an he's the man who wrote the song ah was singin to yoose!'

Jock began reciting 'Wee Willie Winkie' again, all the time trying to put the boys at their ease by smiling as heartily at them as he could. The lads were now halfway back to the bridge, their escape route from this spectre with iron teeth. They turned and ran for their lives.

Old Jock gave up singing the familiar rhyme. He watched as the two nippers disappeared off through the carved angels and ancient tombstones of the Necropolis. The September breeze made the old man shiver. Jock descended down through the City of the Dead, it was time to get himself warmed up in one of his favourite haunts along the High Street and he definitely needed a wee dram to calm his nerves after all the excitement.

The two boys ran as fast as they could down the street, dodging in and out of people who were hurrying home from their work. They managed to catch their breath as they waited to cross the busy intersection at the Gallowgate. When they reached the familiar territory of Glasgow Green, the pair stopped for a rest next to the River Clyde. A bunch of kids from their neighbourhood were just finishing a game of football on the Green. Tam and Robbie ran to meet their friends and the story of their near escape from the Necropolis poured out of them. A crowd had soon gathered around the youngsters, who enjoyed exaggerating the horror and terror of their near miss with a walking corpse. By the time all of the children were back in their homes for tea, the story of the walking dead man with iron teeth (Old Jock!) had spread among the youth of the Gorbals and Hutchestown, both very densely populated parts of the city.

Later that evening, around dusk, as the street lamps were flickering into life, casting white pools of light on pavements and tenements, children began to congregate in back courts and street corners. Planks of wood, tree branches, brush poles, stones in old socks, empty lemonade bottles, chunks of broken kerb stones, and rusty bits of broken iron railings were among the primitive weapons being distributed amongst the youths. The news had spread like wildfire that a vampire with iron teeth had killed and eaten two wee boys in the Gorbals Necropolis. An army of up to one hundred weans marched to the old graveyard in the heart of the Gorbals. This was the Southern Necropolis, not the same as the one that Tam and Robbie had visited earlier that day, in the north of Glasgow. Children came from all over the area. The tightly packed tenement closes and backcourts were like a rabbit warren conducive to an efficient early warning communications system. Bigger boys arrived at the cemetery first, and set off through the huge granite slabs of tombstones and undergrowth, slashing through the brambles with their sticks and weapons. Younger children followed closely behind, looking nervously over their shoulders lest they should be struck by the fiend from behind. The hunt was on; no vampire was going to kill their cousins and terrorise this city, especially not one with iron teeth.

When Constable Deeprose arrived at the Southern Necropolis, he was expecting to find some empty paint pots and graffiti. The call had come into the station about a disturbance and kids in the old Victorian cemetery. No one at the station was surprised by this, there had been vandalism here before, paint daubed on the walls, and gravestones pushed over, just the way kids were these days. As he entered through the gates, nothing could have prepared him for the bizarre scene he witnessed that night. The skyline lit up with a red and orange glow from nearby steelworks, Dixon's Blazes, and the shadows of gravestones, trees and kids danced eerily around the Southern Necropolis. He shone his torch over the gang of children, who swarmed towards him all shouting and yelling at the same time. When he was surrounded by the flock of miniature vigilantes, he managed to make out what they were saying – had he seen the seven foot vampire with the iron teeth? The one that had killed two wee boys? Deeprose rounded the children up and assured them that no children had been killed by vampires that night. As he walked out of the old kirkyard, he felt like the Pied Piper of Hamlyn leading a train of hypnotised bairns. With the mob dispersed and off to their respective homes, the constable locked the gate and went back to the station, where he filed one of the strangest reports on record.

The rumours hadn't quite been quelled though, as another mob of weapon-wielding kids returned to the cemetery the following night. They were still looking for the vampire. The police locked the gate securely after the second night. They even had to reassure worried adults that no children had been killed by vampires in Glasgow that week, let alone that century. The world media picked up on these incidents and made it a global story. They blamed American comic books for warping children's minds and leading to mass hysteria. But we know the truth: 'Jenny wi the airn teeth' was the real culprit that September evening in 1954.

STORY SOURCES AND NOTES

THE UPPER WARD

Cowdaily Castle

Jennifer Westwood and Sophia Kingshill, *The Lore of Scotland: A Guide to Scottish Legends* (Arrow Books, 2011), Couthalley Castle, pp. 176–177.

Robert Chambers, *Popular Rhymes of Scotland*, New Edition (4th) (London and Edinburgh, 1826), pp. 336–337.

Hugh Quiglay, *Lanarkshire in Prose and Verse: The County Anthologies No. 2* (Lanarkshire, 1929), p. 38.

Michael Scot and His Industrious Imps

Ed Archer, Paul Archibald and Margaret Davis, *Historical Clydesdale: Parish by Parish, Lanark* (Lanark & District Archaeological Society, 2016), p. 92.

Jennifer Westwood and Sophia Kingshill, *The Lore of Scotland: A Guide to Scottish Legends* (London: Arrow Books, 2011), p. 171.

The Brownie of Dolphinton Mill

Katharine Briggs, *The Fairies in Tradition and Literature* (London and New York: Routledge, 2002), p. 39.

Jennifer Westwood and Sophia Kingshill, *The Lore of Scotland: A Guide to Scottish Legends* (London: Arrow Books, 2011), p. 180.

Murder on Libberton Moor

George Paul, *Another Look at Carnwath* (Lanark: Thomas Houston & Co. Ltd, 1989), pp. 18–21.

Jennifer Westwood and Sophia Kingshill, *The Lore of Scotland: A Guide to Scottish Legends* (London: Arrow Books, 2011), pp. 174–175.

The Fairies of Merlin's Crag
Katharine M. Briggs, *A Dictionary of British Folk-Tales, Part B. Folk Legends* (London and New York: Routledge, 1970), pp. 215–217.
Judy Paterson, *Scottish Folk Tales for Children* (Cheltenham: The History Press, 2017), 'The Orra Man', pp. 30–41.
R. Macdonald Robertson, *Selected Highland Folktales* (David St John Publisher, reprinted, 1993), 'Duncan Fraser and the Fairies', pp. 10–12.
Although there is no Merlin's Crag in Lanarkshire today, there is an Arthur's Crag in the Clyde Valley and a Fairy Hill in Carmyle. Perhaps the story was originally attached to one of these locations.

The Oldest Man in Scotland
The Rev. J. Moir Porteous, *God's Treasure house in Scotland: A History of Times, Mines and Lands in the Southern Highlands* (London: Simpkin, Marshall & Co.; Edinburgh & Glasgow: John Menzies & Co. 1876), pp. 99–101.
Kenneth Ledger, *This is the Story of John Taylor Who is Buried in Leadhills Graveyard* (https://ledgerkenneth.wixsite.com/leadhills-mines/john-taylor)

Fairy Tales from Douglas
The Scottish Journal of Topography, Antiquities, Traditions, Etc Vol. 1. From September 1847 to February 1848 (Edinburgh: Thomas George Stevenson, John Menzies), p. 150.

Nannie's Invisible Helper
The Scottish Journal of Topography, Antiquities, Traditions, Etc Vol. 1. From September 1847 to February 1848 (Edinburgh: Thomas George Stevenson, John Menzies), p. 150.

The Legend of Cora Linn
Graham's Illustrated Magazine, Vol. X1.1X (Philadelphia, December 1856, No. 6).
History of Lanark, and Guide to the Scenery, 3rd edition (Lanark, 1835).

STORIES AND FOLKLORE FROM LANARK'S CASTLEGATE

William Wallace and Marion Braidfute
Ed Archer on William Wallace in Lanark, Lanark and District Archaeological Society, www.clydesdalesheritage.org.uk, 2014.
Averil Stewart, *The Links of Clyde*, 2nd edition (Wishaw: Press Printing Works, 1945), p. 55.
Hugh Quigley, *Lanarkshire in Prose and Verse: The County Anthologies No. 2* (London, E. Mathews & Marrot,1929), pp. 55–56. Quoting from Blind Harry's poem, 'How Wallace spoke of his Love in Lanark'. Blind Harry's poems were printed in 1510 and are one of the earliest existing accounts of William Wallace.

Daniel Martin, *Upper Clydesdale: A History and a Guide* (Glasgow: Tuckwell Press, 1999), pp. 23–24.

Whuppity Scoorie
Ed Archer, Paul Archibald and Margaret Davis, *Historical Clydesdale: Parish by Parish, Lanark* (Lanark & District Archaeological Society, 2016), pp. 175–176.
Daniel Martin, *Upper Clydesdale: A History and a Guide* (Glasgow: Tuckwell Press, 1999), pp. 37–38.
Jennifer Westwood and Sophia Kingshill, *The Lore of Scotland: A Guide to Scottish Legends* (Reprint, London: Arrow Books, 2011), p. 190.

The Girnin Dog
Paul Archibald, *The Girnin Dug* (printed notes at Lanark Library, 2016).

Wallace and the Wraiths of Clydesdale
The Scottish Journal of Topography, Antiquities, Traditions, Etc Vol. 1. From September 1847 to February 1848. (Edinburgh: Thomas George Stevenson, John Menzies), p. 148.

Katie Neevie's Hoard
Robert Chambers, *Popular Rhymes of Scotland*, New Edition (4th) (London and Edinburgh, 1826), pp. 242–243.
Jennifer Westwood and Sophia Kingshill, *The Lore of Scotland: A Guide to Scottish Legends* (London: Arrow Books, 2011), pp. 41–42.
Hugh Quiglay, *Lanarkshire in Prose and Verse: The County Anthologies No.*

  2 (London, E. Mathews & Marrot, 1929), pp. 40–42.

The Lockharts' Lucky Penny
Katharine M. Briggs, *A Dictionary of British Folk-Tales, Part B. Folk Legends* (London and New York: Routledge, 1970), pp. 88–89.
George Paul, *Another Look at Carnwath,* (Lanark: Thomas Houston & Co. Ltd, 1989), pp. 61–62.
The Scottish Journal of Topography, Antiquities, Traditions, Vol. 1. From September 1847, to February 1848. (Edinburgh: Thomas George Stevenson, John Menzies), pp. 72–73.
Andy Hunter, *The Lee Penny,* (Tells the story on YouTube, www.youtube.com/watch?v=da2s6XDJNGQ) June 2011.

The Black Clydesdale Horse
Charlotte Howat, oral source – I recorded Charlotte telling me this story about one of her father's horses, Queenie, on 15 February 2010. Sadly Charlotte passed in April 2013. She is missed terribly by her family and everyone who knew her – she was a very natural and entertaining storyteller with a heart of gold.

THE MIDDLE WARD

The Blue Flame of Strathaven

Thomas Eric Niven, *East Kilbride: The History of Parish and Village,* 2nd edition (Glasgow: Gavin Watson Ltd, 1965, 1988) 'The Lowe O'Carnduff', p. 124.

Jennifer Westwood and Sophia Kingshill, *The Lore of Scotland: A Guide to Scottish Legends* (London: Arrow Books, 2011), p. 203.

Sita, the Indian Princess of Larkhall

Christine Frew, *Ghost Stories from the Clyde Valley* (Clyde Valley Tourist Board, 1987), pp. 12–13.

James Robertson, *Scottish Ghost Stories* (New York: Warner Books, reprinted 1997), pp. 162–178.

Lily Seafield, *Scottish Ghosts* (New Lanark: Lomond Books, Geddes & Grosset, 2002), pp. 106–107.

www.hiddenglasgow.com/forums/viewtopic.php?t=3081 (2/10/17) The Black Lady of Broomhill House, Larkhall. A Ghost Story by Sheepdug. (13/11/2005).

Cadzow Oaks

www.cadzowhistory.org/cadzow-a-short-history

A story by Ian Hamilton QC – originally printed in *The Scottish Banner* newspaper, July 1996.

Historical sources state that Robert the Bruce bestowed the barony of Cadzow upon Walter Fitz Gilbert. I have used the name Alan Fitz Walter in keeping with the story related to Ian Hamilton by his father, my original source.

The Curling Warlock of Mains Castle

'Magic Torch', *Tales of the Oak* (Greenock, 2006) pp. 126–130 – 'Auld Dunrod/Cold Heart. The Ballad of Auld Dunrod', pp. 132–134.

Iain MacDonald, *Murder at the Mains,* Script (Copy at Hamilton Library, South Lanarkshire)

Averil Stewart, *The Links of Clyde,* 2nd edition (Wishaw: Press Printing Works, 1941) p. 54.

Alexander Crawford Lindsay Earl of Crawford, *Lives of the Lindsays: Or, A Memoir of the Houses of Crawford and Balcarres,* Vol. 1 (John Murray: London, Albemarie Street, 1849).

Tibbie, the Witch of Kirktonholme

Thomas. Eric Niven, *East Kilbride: The History of Parish and Village,* 2nd edition (Glasgow: Gavin Watson Ltd, 1965, 1988), p. 149.

The Tale of Kate Dalrymple

A traditional song written by William Watt a handloom weaver from East Kilbride (1792–1859).

Finlay Forbes, 'Who Was Kate Dalrymple?' (Box and Fiddle Archive, November 2005)

https://boxandfiddlearchive.weebly.com/who-was-kate-dalrymple.html
(5/7/20)

'The Corries', Kate Dalrymple (YouTube.com, 4 October 2006)
www.youtube.com/watch?v=lKmPxLkSqv8 (5/7/2020)

Bartram, the Giant of Shotts
Jennifer Macfadyen, *Bertram de Shotts* (Doorstep History, 5 June 2012)
    https://doorstephistory.wordpress.com/tag/bertram-de-shotts
Averil Stewart, *The Links of Clyde* 2nd edition (Wishaw: Press Printing
    Works, 1945), pp. 81–82.
Maxine Ross, *The Legend of the Giant, Bertram De Shotts and William
    Muirhead of Lauchope* http://fluffylemonde.blogspot.com/2016/ 18
    December 2016.
'The Muirhead Legends – The Killing of Bartram Shotts'
https://www.motherbedford.com/Muirhead/Muirhead000.htm

The White Hare
William Erskine, *The Book of Airdrie: Being a Composite Picture of the
    Life of a Scottish Burgh by Its Inhabitants*, edited by James K. Scobbie
    (Glasgow,Jackson, Son and Co., 1954), pp. 251–253.
Erskine, William, 'The White Hare: A Monkland Legend', *Airdrie and
    Coatbridge Advertiser*, 24 February 1940.
There is a similar story about an unlucky white hare and the Monkland
    estate in a much older issue of the newspaper: T'he Lover's Leap: A
    Monkland Legend', *Airdrie and Coatbridge Advertiser*, 24 January
    1891.

Maggie Ramsay: The Witch of Auld Airdrie
William Erskine, *The Book of Airdrie: Being a Composite Picture of the
    Life of a Scottish Burgh by its Inhabitants*, edited by James K. Scobbie
    (Glasgow,Jackson, Son and Co., 1954), pp. 253–257.
Erskine, William, 'The Legend of Maggie Ramsay', *Airdrie and
    Coatbridge Advertiser,* 5 August 1944.

When the Devil Helped with Airdrie's Harvest
William Erskine, *The Book of Airdrie: Being a Composite Picture of the
    Life of a Scottish Burgh by its Inhabitants*, edited by James K. Scobbie
    (Glasgow,Jackson, Son and Co., 1954), pp. 249–251.
Erskine, William, 'When the De'il Helpit Wi' Airdrie's Haurvest', *Airdrie
    and Coatbridge Advertiser,* 21 November 1942.

THE LOWER WARD

The Rutherglen Bannock
F. Marian McNeill, *The Silver Bough Vol. 3: A Calendar of Scottish
    National Festivals: Halloween to Yule* (Glasgow: Beith Printing Co. Ltd;
    Aldershot: Stuart Titles Ltd, 1990), pp. 21–24.

David Ure: *The History of Rutherglen and East Kilbride: published With a View to Promote the Study of Antiquity and Natural History* (Glasgow: David Niven, 1793).

A version of the story of The Runaway Bannock exists in almost every collection of Scottish children's folk tales, eg:

Norah and William Montgomerie, *The Well at the World's End and Other Stories* (Edinburgh: Birlinn, 2013),'The Wee Bannock', Ayrshire, pp. 92–95.

Saint Kentigern, the Patron Saint of Glasgow, How Mungo Came to Glasgow and The Battle between Morken and Kentigern

Adam Ardrey, *Finding Merlin: The Truth Behind the Legend* (Edinburgh: Mainstream Publishing Company, 2007).

Geoff Holder, *The Guide to Mysterious Glasgow* (Cheltenham: The History Press, 2009), pp. 159–165.

Andrew Wallace, *Popular Traditions of Glasgow: Historical, Legendary and Biographical* (Glasgow: Thomas D. Morison; London: Hamilton, Adams & Co., 1889).

Aberdeen Breviary, *The Legends & Communications & Celebrations of St Kentigern his Friends and Disciples translated from the Aberdeen Breviary & the Anglo-Saxon Chronicle*, trans. James Ingram (London: Everyman Press, 1912).

Cynthia Whiddon Green, *Jocelyn, a Monk of Furness: The Life of Kentigern (Mungo)*. As part of MA Thesis at University of Houston, December, 1998. Fordham University granted permission to reproduce: https://sourcebooks.fordham.edu/basis/Jocelyn-LifeofKentigern.asp

The Fish and the Ring

Hamilton District: A History (Hamilton District Libraries, 1995).
    Note: This was a reprint of a much older book, and the only source that places the story of The Fish and the Ring in the royal hunting grounds of Cadzow. It does make more sense that the King and his Queen spent their leisure time hunting, flirting and fishing in the lush forests and fields of Cadzow, rather than the busy centre of Glasgow.

In the story map this story is number 28 and situated in the Middle Ward, where most of the action takes place.

The Witches of Pollok

Thomas Davidson, *Rowan Tree and Red Thread: A Scottish Witchcraft Miscellany, Tales, Legends and Ballads together with a Description of the Witches Rites and Ceremonies* (Edinburgh and London: Oliver & Boyd, 1949), pp. 115–128.

Geoff Holder, *Paranormal Glasgow* (Cheltenham: The History Press, 2011), pp. 53–64.

Ron Halliday, *Haunted Glasgow* (Glasgow: Bell and Bain Ltd, 2008), pp. 126–132.

The Scottish Storytelling Centre is delighted to be associated with the *Folk Tales* series developed by The History Press. Its talented storytellers continue the Scottish tradition, revealing the regional riches of Scotland in these volumes. These include the different environments, languages and cultures encompassed in our big wee country. The Scottish Storytelling Centre provides a base and communications point for the national storytelling network, along with national networks for Traditional Music and Song and Traditions of Dance, all under the umbrella of TRACS (Traditional Arts and Culture Scotland). See www.scottishstorytellingcentre.co.uk for further information. The Traditional Arts community of Scotland is also delighted to be working with all the nations and regions of Great Britain and Ireland through the *Folk Tales* series.

Donald Smith
Director, Tracs
Traditional Arts and Culture Scotland

The Sheep's Heid

John Simpson, *A History of Govan* (Sponsored by the Govan Fair Association, 1983), p. 29.

Geoff Holder, *The Guide to Mysterious Glasgow* (Cheltenham: The History Press, 2009), pp. 157–158.

The Govan Cat

John Simpson, *A History of Govan* (Sponsored by the Govan Fair Association, 1983), pp. 22–23.

Geoff Holder, *The Guide to Mysterious Glasgow* (Cheltenham: The History Press, 2009), p. 160, quoting Ray McKenzie (*Sculpture in Glasgow*).

The Vampire with the Iron Teeth

Geoff Holder, *Paranormal Glasgow* (Cheltenham: The History Press, 2011), pp. 71–79.

Geoff Holder, *The Guide to Mysterious Glasgow* (Cheltenham: The History Press, 2009), pp. 153–154.

Sandy Hobbs in Jennifer Westwood and Sophia Kingshill, *The Lore of Scotland: A Guide to Scottish Legends,* (London: Arrow Books, 2011), pp. 186–187.

The destination for history
www.thehistorypress.co.uk